Expanding on the metaphor of weeds in the garden used by Jesus in Mark 4, Gretchen weaves together personal stories and Scriptural references with her clinical insight to create a book that is a must read for anyone who desires to grow in their spiritual journey.

—Kimberly Baldwin, M.A., L.P.C.
(Licensed Professional Counselor)

Attitude is everything! *The Journey Out* explores the origin of negative attitudes and directs you in overcoming your hindrances to healthy personal growth. Read it, do it, and enjoy a fresh view of life and growth in your relationships!

—Richard Powell, Associate Pastor
Smoky Hill Vineyard, SHV Care

Are you in a spiritual rut? There may be a very good reason. *The Journey Out* will help you determine why you are stuck, and more importantly, how to get unstuck. It explores the Scripture for its answers, and you may be surprised to find out what it has to say about your life. *The Journey Out* tills the Scripture to reveal the places we often get stuck, and more importantly, the way out.

—Matt Dobschuetz
Living Waters Ministry Coordinator
Vineyard Christian Church of Evanston

Gretchen is a woman of conviction and tender heart. Through her professional insight and personal stories, Gretchen reveals what the Lord has sown, weeded out, and harvested in her life. Read this book, and let it instruct, exhort, and encourage yo

—Nancy Lee, Avi

the JOURNEY OUT

the JOURNEY OUT

OVERCOMING Attitudes
That Hinder Our Spiritual Growth

*To Isaac —
I love you! Thank You So
much for all of your help
and support on this
project! ♥ Gretchen*

GRETCHEN FLORES, MA, LCPC
LICENSED CLINICAL PROFESSIONAL COUNSELOR

Pleasant W rd
A Division of WINEPRESS PUBLISHING

Pleasant Word (a division of WinePress Publishing, PO Box 428, Enumclaw, WA 98022) functions only as book publisher. As such, the ultimate design, content, editorial accuracy, and views expressed or implied in this work are those of the author.

ISBN 13: 978-1-4141-1156-8
ISBN 10: 1-4141-1156-8
Library of Congress Catalog Card Number: 2007910288

To God, who has led me through this Journey
and
To my husband, Isaac—I love you
and
Jacob and Hannah—you are wonderful.

CONTENTS

ACKNOWLEDGMENTS

THERE IS ABSOLUTELY no way that I can give credit to everyone that I have learned from, been inspired by, or read from. I have taken numerous classes, seminars, and read many books and Bible studies, and listened to many sermons. I have learned from family, friends, colleagues, and pastors, and I feel it is impossible to credit all of the sources that have contributed to my writing. All I can say is thank you to all of the people who have inspired me to change and grow (including my counselors) and, most of all, to God, my friend and my maker, who has changed me from within with His love. His presence in my life has made all of the difference. I also thank my clients who have allowed me to come alongside of them to support them. I have also learned a great deal from each of you and how you have pressed forward on your own personal journeys.

I thank most of all, my husband, Isaac, for being so steadfast and supportive of me. Thank you also for being patient with "mount wash me" and "mount fold me," pizza nights while I worked on this project, and for helping give the kids baths and taking them places while I worked. You're the best!

I also thank my extended family, who has always been there for me. I am grateful for your presence in my life. Thanks to my mom, who always said to me, "Yes, you can," and who has been an inspiration to me in many ways. Thanks to my dad, who I always love to hang out with and whose input I always love to hear. I appreciate your input and support on this project. Thanks also to my mom-in-law for your help with the kiddos and making "mount fold me" a little more manageable.

I also appreciate honest feedback from my proofreaders. Nancy, thanks for your upfront, constructive feedback. I love an honest suggestion.

To my kids, you are beautiful and wonderful! Thanks for being patient with me while I finished this book. I know sometimes I couldn't play with you because I was working on the book. My favorite thing to do in life is be your mom. I hope that you are inspired by this book someday when you can read. I pray that you will have fruitful lives and have a close relationship with the Lord as you venture on your own journeys!

INTRODUCTION

SINCE CHILDHOOD YOU have desired an occupation. Becoming a firefighter, nurse, doctor, or dancer was your childhood dream. Then, if you went to college, you were asked to declare a major based on what you wanted to do with your life. If you did not go to college, then you chose (or had chosen for you) a trade or skill with which you could learn to be productive and earn an income.

What about your personal or spiritual life? How do you measure productivity in areas that involve more vague or ambiguous measurements? What does it mean to be *fruitful*? Is it attainable for you? What does it even look like? To be fruitful is to be productive, to have an outcome that is tangible. It involves having a *harvest* that is measurable in quantities, much as farmers count barrels of grain or apples.

God urges us to be fruitful, and many of us desire to grow personally and to grow in our faith. *The Journey Out* is about removing what hinders us from growing spiritually so that we can be more fruitful. Our negative attitudes that hinder our spiritual growth are *weeds* that interfere with the growth of the primary fruit-bearing plant or tree that produces a harvest.

Once we can identify the weeds and *pull them* from the soil of our souls, we can grow spiritually. Our positive attitudes have a chance to grow and *bear fruit* in our lives. For some of us, that might mean a *harvest* that we have always desired but that has evaded us. If you have a desire to grow and flourish in your spiritual life, then this book will help you to reach those goals.

Personally, God has done a tremendous healing work in me, and that is most of what inspired this book. Several years ago I had an idea to write about the things that God has taught me in my personal walk with Him. I thought of the name *The Journey Out* as a reflection of my own healing journey out of the weeds and into fruitfulness. It has been amazing to me to see this book becoming a reality as God has urged me on to share outwardly the things I have learned through the presence of the Holy Spirit in my life and through having a willingness to learn.

The lessons I learned, and the attitudes that God has helped me change, are all in this book and are very personal to me, as I have begun to experience greater depth and freedom in my walk of faith and my relationship with the Lord. Of course, I am still a work in progress, and I often fall back into old attitudes that hinder me. But I hope that what I have learned will help others move forward in their relationship with God and into a fruitful life that has a greater freedom from the *weeds* that hinder our growth. If you have a desire to grow and to have a more fruitful life, then it is my hope that this book will inspire you.

Each chapter may appear to stand independently of the others, and it might be tempting to bypass a chapter if you feel it doesn't apply to you. I encourage you to read all of the chapters, even if you may feel they are not a primary concern for you. Each chapter has something unique to offer. The common thread for the chapters is that each area discussed is common to our human predicament in that we all struggle from time to time and to varying degrees with the same issues. We all need growth and God's grace to sustain us as we mature in our faith. Understanding each area also helps us to be sympathetic to those we love who may also struggle with some of these issues.

It is also important to understand that this is a process and that God will still love us when we have weeds and He can still use us. This book is a culmination of many years of personally pressing into God, and I am still growing. The purpose of this book is to increase your spiritual growth and to help free you from attitudes that may be hindering you. Best wishes as you embark on your journey.

CHAPTER 1

THE WEED

DRIVING BY THE side of our home the other day, I noticed that our attractive row of flowering bushes were flourishing nicely, except that one of them had a large weed choking the life out of it. Its growth had been stunted by the weed, and the little purple flowers no longer bloomed. The other three bushes are three times its size and are flourishing beautifully. Later, while doing yard work, my husband pulled the giant weed out and then did an imitation by flexing his muscles and looking down at the poor struggling bush exclaiming, "I will dominate you!" as if he were the weed. We both laughed, because it was obvious that the poor little bush was significantly smaller than the others and was the only bush that did not bear any purple blooms.

SPIRITUAL IMPLICATIONS

Realizing that this has a spiritual application, I considered how often we have "weeds" in our lives that literally choke the life out of us. The weeds choke us emotionally and spiritually and cause us to have stunted personal growth. Not all weeds are the same. Some are large and hearty, others are less obvious, but all weeds compete for space, nutrients, and water, which will interfere with the primary plant's growth. This is also true for our spiritual lives. Problems may interfere with our personal growth to varying degrees. We may or may not be aware of how much they are hindering us, and we may have no clue of how to get rid of them on our own. To some extent there will always be weeds this side of heaven. However, weeds can severely hinder us if we allow certain harmful attitudes or *weeds* to take root in our lives.

Weeds are tenacious and difficult to root out. It is not sufficient to pull a weed out by holding it at its base and removing the top of the plant. It will return. Furthermore, the larger the weed is, the harder it is to extricate the entire root. If you have weeded your yard, then you know that when you pull out a large weed, often part of the root breaks off and stays in the ground. What you need to do is dig out the root with a gardening shovel until it is completely removed in order to prevent it from growing back.

In addition, weeds are full of thorns, burrs, and have been known to change productive land into ineffectual space. Weeds cause damage in more than one way. In addition to competing for nutrients and water, they can also host pests and diseases that can spread to crops and devastate a harvest. They multiply rapidly, either by disseminating seeds by wind or through their root systems. Some weeds can reproduce themselves if only a fragment of the root is left in the ground. Other weeds produce tens of thousands of seeds that can germinate over several seasons, with some seeds remaining dormant for years until they are exposed to the right conditions. Some types of seeds can survive up to 100 years or more, bringing back to life weeds once thought gone. Eradicating such weeds is very difficult and requires hard work and persistence (Weeds, *Wikipedia, the free encyclopedia*).

Again, this has a spiritual application, as we need to recognize that sometimes when working through certain problems, it is not enough to just cover it up, partially deal with it, or worse, ignore it altogether. That is only a temporary solution. The problem will grow until it starts to rob us of God's rich blessings. We need to do the hard work that it takes to dig out the problem from the root. This involves a certain amount of commitment and sometimes emotional pain. However, in the long run, once the root is out and the weed is gone, we are free again to grow and flourish as God designed us to do. When we are free to thrive, we grow in our faith, and we blossom and bear fruit. Our lives begin to produce a healthy harvest, unhindered by weeds that can strangle our personal and spiritual growth. God's Word is the healthy crop in our hearts that produces a harvest.

> Then Jesus said to them, "Don't you understand this parable? How then will you understand any parable? The farmer sows the word. Some people are like seed along the path, where the word is sown. As soon as they hear it, Satan comes and takes away the word that was sown in them. Others, like seed sown on rocky places, hear the word and at once receive it with joy. But since they have no root, they last only a short time. When trouble or persecution comes because of the word, they quickly fall away. Still others, like seed sown among thorns, hear the word; but the worries of this life, the deceitfulness of wealth and the desires for other things come in and choke the word, making it unfruitful. Others, like seed sown on good soil, hear the word, accept it, and produce

a crop—thirty, sixty or even a hundred times what was sown."

—Mark 4:13–20

DESIRE

As believers we want to be fruitful, we want to produce a harvest in our lifetime. Jesus strongly encourages fruitfulness, and He noted that fruit-bearing is a natural occurrence for those who truly believe. Yet, we get bogged down by the worries of this life, and we are tempted by wealth and are distracted by worldly things. We may fail to recognize the weeds that are hindering our spiritual growth and fruitfulness. It is easy to avoid facing chronic problems in our lives, just as we might look at a weed and think, *It really doesn't look that bad, maybe I will just leave it there,* or *I don't have time now, I'll get to it later.* We aren't aware of how much this hinders us.

CO-EXISTENCE

Farmers are aware that many weeds can coexist with a crop for a while before they become truly problematic. Weeds typically don't begin to compete with a crop until three weeks or so into the growing season. As the weeds grow they begin to pull nutrients away from the crop and gradually, over time, pull greater and greater amounts of nutrients (*Wikipedia*). Naively, we allow our weeds to co-exist with us, unaware that they are growing and gaining strength in our lives. That's why Jesus emphasized so strongly that we need to deal with our weeds if we want to be fruitful and if we don't want to lose our faith. Weeds not only hinder our growth, but also they can, if unchecked, pull us away from our life source, Jesus, and cause us to become disheartened and lose faith.

"ATTRACTIVE" WEEDS

In another parallel, some weeds have an attraction of their own, with flowers that are yellow or purple, and they actually look good. My one-year-old daughter was drawn to the yellow dandelions at my son's soccer game. While he was busy playing soccer, my daughter was cruising around picking the yellow tops and handing them to parents at the field as a little gift that they "oohed" and "ahhed" over. Even so, if weeds are allowed to grow, they will eventually choke out the grass and continue to multiply many yards or miles away from their source. More importantly for the farmer producing a crop, the removal of weeds is critical to insure a healthy and plentiful crop harvest.

Similarly, we may see *weeds* in our life, but don't recognize the threat they create because they don't look so bad. They seem neutral or insignificant. They seem to linger on the fringes but aren't yet interfering with our daily life. We don't realize that they need to be addressed so that we can reach our potential, or in some cases, avoid disaster. We often become accustomed to the weeds being there, so we aren't alarmed by their presence. However, many of us encounter similar problems again and again. When that happens, it is a signal that you are running into a spiritual weed that needs to be dug out so that you can find the freedom in your life that God intends for you, because, "It is for freedom that Christ has set us free" (Gal. 5:1).

It is tempting to wait for others to address their own weeds or problems. It's easier to see the problems that other people have and complain about how that is affecting you. Someone once told me that the things that bother you the most in others are often the things you struggle with yourself. Many times this is true. The first step to dealing with our weeds is being able to see them for what they are.

Then, and only then, are we able to start to take the steps we need to root them out. Some are easy to pull out, and others take more work.

WEED REMOVAL

Although weeds are difficult to eradicate, it is not impossible. Today we have many methods of weed control, including pesticides. However, plowing them out is still one of the most effective methods if you do not want to use chemicals. Tilling the soil to uproot the weeds from deep down in the ground causes the weeds to die. It can also help rid the area of other pests. The farmer plows during an off season, and he will refrain from planting a crop until the plowing has been completed.

As believers, we go through what many call *seasons* in our spiritual growth. It is important to allow God to do the plowing work in our hearts and minds in order to bear the most productive harvest later on. It is tempting to skip the hard work of weeding and tilling the soil of your soul, but it needs to be done if you want to be fruitful. Can you embrace this process? Are you willing to endure it?

Allow God to plow out the weeds in your life. It is by His mercy and love for you that He takes out the weeds. We often resist it because many of us have developed an affinity for our weeds. We need to be willing to "throw off everything that hinders and the sin that so easily entangles, and let us run with perseverance the race marked out for us" (Heb. 12:1). Our enemy plants the weeds and distracts us so we don't notice them. In facing this important task, you may find that you encounter a lot of resistance and struggle. But I think you will find it a worthwhile endeavor to endure, because surely once the weeds are pulled out by the root, you can grow and flourish and find freedom again.

REGAINING STRENGTH

Now that the gigantic choking weed has been pulled out of the ground next to the flowering bush in our yard, I am pretty sure we will see it start to grow and, hopefully, start to catch up to the other three bushes. Even a few weeks later, some new, little flowers have begun to peek out. So now, instead of failing to thrive, the little bush is starting to regain its strength and come back to life. In our lives, once the weeds are gone, we can experience true growth rather than stunted growth, or withering away, just barely making it through. Sometimes we blame God that we are stuck, but we fail to recognize that we need to "weed our garden" before we can start to grow again.

In Scripture, Jesus discussed the problem of weeds in His parables as a spiritual metaphor, as not only problematic for farmers but also for our spiritual growth as well. The following verse illustrates:

> Jesus told them another parable: "The kingdom of heaven is like a man who sowed good seed in his field. But while everyone was sleeping, his enemy came and sowed weeds among the wheat, and went away. When the wheat sprouted and formed heads, then the weeds also appeared. The owner's servants came to him and said, 'Sir, didn't you sow good seed in your field? Where then did the weeds come from?' 'An enemy did this,' he replied."
>
> —Matthew 13:24–28

The *good seed* has great potential in our life that many of us have not yet fully experienced. If the good seed that the Lord planted in our lives, with the intention that it grow good fruit, gets choked out by the weeds the enemy has planted, we won't get to experience fruit-bearing. We must be willing to allow the Master Gardener to come and pull out the weeds so that our lives might produce a harvest. Our lives can be fruitful. We can experience spiritual growth that allows us to have joy in life beyond the mundane tasks. We can bear blossoms that make our life much more interesting and hopeful.

Are there weeds choking out your enjoyment of life? Is your marriage suffering? Are you hurting and don't know why? Do you feel stuck? Trapped? Are you ready and willing to pursue change? Allow Jesus to come alongside you and help you to grow and get rid of the weeds that pull spiritual nutrition from your soul. "Then the land will yield its harvest, and God, our God, will bless us" (Ps. 67:6).

CHAPTER 2

THE WEED OF PERFECTIONISM VS. THE FRUIT OF TRUST

Perfectionism—Rigorous rejection of anything less than perfect. Demand for exactness and precision in the completion of tasks or accuracy in all important details.

—*Wikipedia*

BOSSES LOVE PERFECTIONISTS. They come early, stay late, and are eager to please. They do their job well. I hope that some professionals strive for near perfection in their work. For example, I would hope that my heart surgeon, who will be fixing my heart during surgery, is very good at what he does. Yet, even heart surgeons will tell you there are risks which include the fact that they are human, and therefore, not perfect.

Striving to do well in the tasks we have before us is a good thing to do. Doing well helps us to feel productive, to be employable, and to manage our homes and our lives. However, when compulsive perfectionism plagues our every action and reflects how we feel about ourselves, we can

9

severely undermine our enjoyment of life. Perfectionists often only feel good about themselves when the outcome of their efforts is "right" or "perfect." What makes this so challenging to the perfectionist is that it is never quite good enough, so they will continue to strive and strive until they are out of time or exhausted in their efforts to perfect their work. Then they may apologize profusely for their imperfections, much to the annoyance of their friends and family members who see that they have indeed gone above and beyond what is expected.

Pervading many areas of their life, work, family, relationships, and home life, the thoughts of the perfectionist demand that if it's not perfect, then it is horrible. Things are seen in extremes of *"all-or-nothing"* thinking. For example, the perfectionist will feel extremely anxious about a project because deep down they feel, *I'm either all good or all bad, but nothing in between.* If the project doesn't meet expectations, the individual will see it as a complete failure. The perfectionist sees actions and outcomes as a reflection of how they feel about themselves. If it is not "perfect," then the perfectionist will feel bad, due to an inability to separate identity, or *self*, from tasks. This can be extremely debilitating, especially when self-imposed standards are excessive.

To some degree, we all care about what other people think of us. Even when we say we don't care, we probably do care in that it would feel good to know that others think well of us. This is normal, and to some extent, healthy, because God created us as social beings who are intended to be in relationship with each other and with Him. However, if we feel deeply insecure about ourselves and rely on what others think of us or on external sources of self esteem, then we are left to toss about in waves of uncertainty. We can shift frequently in our moods due to our perceived or real feedback from others.

PERFECTIONIST THOUGHT PATTERNS

A perfectionist might ask, "What's wrong with being a perfectionist? I do everything right and on time and better than everyone else." It is not the fact that you do things well that is the problem. It is the stress that it causes. Often, areas of dysfunction in our lives have an inner voice or language of their own that we may or may not be aware of. The inner voice of a perfectionist goes something like this: *I should always be nice and pleasant to everyone, or they may not like me and that would be horrible,* or *I must always be competent at my job or I am not worth much.* This type of inner language may drive us to work past our physical and emotional limits or to deny our own needs in exchange for praise from others.

Other perfectionists set up standards that have to do with income. *I have to make X amount of money or I am not worthwhile. I will do whatever it takes to make sure it happens.* They may subconsciously view situations in all or nothing terms and tell themselves, *If it's not perfect, then I have failed. I am not good at anything...* The perfectionist might say this just after doing an excellent job on something. The focus is on what didn't go as planned, and the result is emotional strife and a drive to do better beyond normal limits of time, fatigue, and reason.

TWO SIDES OF THE COIN

There are two sides of the coin with regard to perfectionism. A perfectionist will either strive endlessly to please others and to meet an unrealistically high standard they have set for themselves, or they may shut down and give up since perfectionists feel that if it is not perfect, it is not worth trying (even if they are unaware that this is what they are feeling). Appearing unmotivated, they may have just given up on themselves and have developed an "I don't care" attitude. If someone feels like a constant failure, they may be prone to surrender to the feeling that they cannot measure up. They will resign themselves to the only other option they feel they have—to give up trying. Some of us may swing back and forth between the extremes of excessive striving and giving up.

My son struggled when he started his soccer program when he was just three years old. I could not understand why he kept giving up. He would start every practice enthusiastic about playing soccer at the field. He looked adorable in all of his soccer gear. We even made sure he had the soccer uniform so he would feel part of the team. Yet, week after week he would play for about five minutes and then stubbornly decide he was done. He would sit on the sidelines and beg to go home.

I tried to say everything I could to encourage him to play, and even bribed him with toys and French fries on the way home. Still, it didn't work, and I was baffled, until I realized that at three years of age he was already a perfectionist. The moment he made a mistake, he decided he was done and parked himself on the sidelines. I started to give him a pep talk on the way to soccer, and his mantra became: "I am going to mess up! But it's okay!" It worked. He started to enjoy playing, and when he fell down or made a mistake, he learned it was all part of the process, and he kept on playing and having fun.

When an individual gives up, that individual may feel deep down that he or she will never meet his or her own standards, or in many cases, his or her parents' standards. This may even be difficult to verbalize or admit, since you may not even be fully aware of it. You are aware that you feel poorly about yourself, and often you are even depressed about your perceived inability to meet your internalized extreme standards.

ORIGINS OF PERFECTIONISM

Because I am a counselor, I feel it is important to understand the source of a problem. There are different reasons why people develop this problem. One is that parents withhold praise or affection from their children. It can happen when parents focus on a child's output over relationship. For example, a parent may only pay attention to a child when it is time for grades to be evaluated, and then the only acceptable grades are all A's.

Other times, certain personality types are more naturally prone to perfectionism because they are eager to please and like doing well. For this reason, it is important to instill in our children the experience that they are loved and accepted apart from their performance. This can be done with a hug or an "I love you" without also adding, "So did you get an A in school today?"

In extreme cases, perfectionism can lead to depression and suicidal thoughts when the individual feels worthless, unless he or she can meet an unrealistic standard he or she feels is impossible to meet. This might be the student who attempts suicide after failing a test, or a man who feels suicidal after losing his job. The individual has cornered themselves in a "lose/lose" situation in which they are trapped inside a box of excessive expectations. They don't see other options. How tragic it is to lose so much hope over an internal expectation that is void of God's grace and love. *God loves us deeply apart from what we do,* and it is important to grasp that this means we can be free from impossible expectations, because God's only hope is that we love Him back.

CULTURAL PROBLEM

This can also be a cultural problem. Some cultures push their children to unrealistically high standards. High expectations can be individual or set up by a family. The result is the same. When children feel unable to meet unrealistically high standards or feel that their output is more valuable than they are, then a deep-rooted complex is developed that carries into adulthood and can be passed from generation to generation. The best way to break this pattern is through surrender to God's love and an understanding of His grace. "The grace of our Lord was poured out on me abundantly, along with the faith and love that is in Christ Jesus" (1 Tim. 1:14). God's gives us His grace, meaning He gives us His favor. It is a free gift and is not contingent on what we do or how well we do it. If we are accustomed to feeling that love is based on our accomplishments, we will struggle to understand God's grace. It is truly a free gift of God's love.

GENERATIONAL PERFECTIONISM

Perfectionism may go back several generations and requires some shifts in thinking to change the pattern. Relationally, perfectionists are often hard on others because they are hard on themselves. Because perfectionists are hard on themselves, they are often unable to see that their standards are excessive and harsh. High and unbending standards are normal for them, as that is either how they were raised or what their personality naturally strives for, or both.

In addition, perfectionist parents often see their children in a perspective that is co-dependent. Co-dependency is an emotional view of others as an extension of one's self. They are, therefore, unable to separate their children's performance from their own. How harshly parents react to children's mistakes may reflect how they feel about themselves. If perfectionist parents won't tolerate those mistakes in themselves, they often won't be tolerated in their children. Parents may unwittingly harm their children's emotional security by pushing them to succeed while withholding love and affection. This is part of the reason perfectionism is learned and passed on to children and children's children. Children look to their parents as mirrors who reflect back if they are acceptable or not. When we communicate to our children that they are not good enough apart from accomplishments, children often will develop perfectionist tendencies.

Breaking the Pattern

The way to begin to change this pattern is to start recognizing your own extreme thoughts and start working toward a healthier balance. We must see our self-esteem from God's perspective rather than from external sources. Looking toward our earthly parents will give us a flawed reflection. In contrast, when we look to our heavenly Father, who truly is perfect and loves us completely as we are, we are able to see a more accurate reflection of who we are. "I praise you because I am fearfully and wonderfully made; your works are wonderful, I know that full well" (Ps. 139:14). In this psalm it is clear that we are considered *wonderful* because we are God's workmanship. We resist that truth because we are accustomed to our faults. But when we recognize that God sees past our faults and loves us as we are, it can transform us. Do you realize that God loves you deeply the way you are, apart from what you do?

The world will tell you to look within yourself and to give yourself affirmations that possibly you never received as a child. Truthfully, I don't think this is all bad. Some of us need to hear the affirmations we weren't given, or were given inconsistently, as a child. However, receiving human affirmations lacks an important ingredient, and that is God's love and grace for us expressed through His Word and His Holy Spirit.

We can tell ourselves that we are acceptable, but often we aren't convinced on our own. The love of God expressed through His Holy Spirit changes us from within, and we begin to know and understand that we are acceptable, and we are loved. "May our Lord Jesus Christ Himself and God our Father, who loved us and by his grace gave us eternal encouragement and good hope, encourage your hearts and strengthen you in every good deed and word" (2 Thess. 2:16–17). God longs for us to understand how deeply He loves us. He strengthens us and encourages us, because He loves us apart from what we do and how well we do it.

ENDLESS PATTERN

In an effort to escape deep-rooted feelings of worthlessness, perfectionists learn that if they please others with their hard work, or if they see that they can accomplish something, then they feel a little bit better about themselves. Unfortunately, it is usually only a short-term solution, and the next task needs to be done, and the next standard needs to be met. Managing uncompromising, lofty standards can be exhausting and stressful over time, since the standard tends to get higher and more unattainable. At the same time, our need for love and acceptance is not satisfied. We finish one task and then go on to the next in a futile cycle that leaves us still feeling empty...and the cycle continues.

HOPE FOR PERFECTIONISTS

Fortunately, we don't have to be controlled by our perfectionism. We can choose a better way. We can be "transformed by the renewing of [our] mind" (Rom. 11:34). First we must recognize and acknowledge that we are not perfect and never will be. Only God is perfect. When we fully understand and accept this truth, we are able to change and grow.

> *He* is the Rock, *His* works are perfect, and all *His* ways are just. A faithful God who does no wrong, upright and just is *He*.
> —Deuteronomy 32:4 (emphasis added)

It is critical for us to grasp and accept what it means that only God is perfect. Only God has what it takes to be perfect. A number of years ago, God convicted me that my perfectionism was driving me to be something I'm not and can never be without God. In a sense, if we devote a majority of our time to it, it becomes an idol before God. When we are trapped in our perfectionism, we fail to step back and allow God to do His work in our lives. We need to accept our imperfections and understand that they are there to draw us closer to God. We fail to receive God's gift of grace because we think we need to do it all on our own efforts.

Perfectionism is, at its core, a signal of distrust in God, and a need to be in control of our own lives. It pushes God aside and says, "I can do it better." It isolates us from others and from God, because it communicates, "I don't need God's help," or "I will do it all, because I am the only one who can do it right." Essentially, it is a refusal to receive God's grace. "Those who cling to worthless idols forfeit the grace that could be theirs" (Jonah 2:8). I don't want to miss out on any of God's grace, because I know that I need it.

God's grace releases us from the pressure to do it all and to have to do it "right." Unfortunately, we are often striving to meet the unrealistically high standards of our parents or of our culture and of trying desperately to please others. We fail to recognize that we please God not by how well we do things, but by our faith. "Without faith it is impossible to please God because anyone who comes to him must believe that he exists and that he rewards those who earnestly seek him" (Heb. 11:6). He is pleased by our faith in Him and, not by how perfectly we do things.

We need to repent of our reliance on self and of our insecurities. God said that we are "fearfully and wonderfully made" (Ps. 139:14). So who are we to say that we are unacceptable to God? He loves us just as we are, and He wants us to trust Him.

> It is God who arms me with strength and makes my way perfect. *He* makes my feet like the feet of a deer; *He* enables me to stand on the heights. *He* trains my hands for battle; my arms can bend a bow of bronze. *You* give me your shield of victory; *you* stoop down to make me great. *You* broaden the path beneath me, so that my ankles do not turn.
> —2 Samuel 22:33–37 (emphasis added)

Notice in the above passage that the author understands that it is God who enables him to be perfect. It is God who strengthens him. God's grace will fill in the gaps if we allow Him to do so. When we are in a loving relationship with God, then we can learn to trust Him enough to lean on Him and allow Him to be our strength.

TRUST GOD

Some of us may be at different places in our faith. If you only know Him as a distant God, then this information has limited value. If He is distant, then saying, "Give your cares to God," is about as meaningless as saying, "Give your cares to that lamppost." The truth is that God is not distant. He is near, and He lives in our heart, if we invite Him in. You cannot get much closer than having God live in your heart. (See Ps. 119:151; Ps. 145:18; Phil. 4:5).

Jesus asks us to trust Him: "Do not let your hearts be troubled. Trust in God; trust also in me" (John 14:1). God has proven trustworthy in my life as I have given my troubles to Him. I am changed into a new person. It is important to confess our lack of trust, because many of us have been sorely disappointed by people in our lives whom we have trusted. We may be completely unaware that we have vowed we will never trust again. Yet, God is trustworthy. "Those who know your name will trust in you, for you, LORD, have never forsaken those who seek you" (Ps. 9:10).

If you have not yet taken the step of faith to trust in Him as your Savior and would like to invite Him into your heart, please take the time to do that right now. Turn to the addendum in the back to follow the prayer for receiving Jesus.

GOD ACCEPTS US

As I stated earlier, perfectionism is often rooted in deep insecurity within ourselves. If we really stop to look inward, we can often find that we look to perfectionism to solve our insecurities, instead of looking to God who shows us that He loves us unconditionally. His acceptance is not based on what we do and how well we do it. If we look to the outcome of our tasks to base our worth on rather than God's

19

grace and love, we will constantly be frustrated, hurting, and feeling bad about ourselves.

We also need to grasp how fully God loves us apart from how well we do what we are doing. When we start to get that, really get that, the anxiety begins to dissipate, and we can accept our imperfections and realize that God's grace is sufficient for us (see 2 Cor. 12:9). God's grace is sufficient for us when we make mistakes, when we hurt someone else's feelings, when we get fired from our job, when we miss an appointment, when we struggle to discipline our children. Accepting our imperfections leads us to understand that we need God's grace that He longs to extend to us. He is a loving God, not a harsh and critical one. He does not look down at you sternly saying, "You didn't do it right." He loves you completely as you are—as imperfect and messy as you are. Reach out to Him, and He will pour out on you His grace and mercy (see Matt. 23:37).

Some of us think we already understand this, and we do. Yet, it is one thing to understand who God is intellectually and another to comprehend Him at an emotional and experiential level in which we feel safe and secure in God's grace and can trust Him to care for us and to carry us when we are lacking. God consistently puts us, His followers, in situations that we aren't able to handle on our own. This gives us an opportunity to exercise our faith and to trust Him. It gives us a chance to allow a loving God to help us when we need Him. That alone can be a great relief and an opportunity for closer reliance and trust in God to meet our needs, which He is not only able to do, but also is something He wants to do. Many of us don't fully comprehend yet that He loves us more than we can imagine. Think about the person you love the most in this life and try to grasp the thought that God loves you more than that...*just as you are.*

OUR THOUGHTS

When we are stuck in perfectionism it can be tremendously helpful to read Scripture verses that remind us of God's love and help. It can also be helpful to use some cognitive therapy techniques. God uses doctors to help us physically, and sometimes, therapists also have ways to help us at a cognitive level. It doesn't mean that we are not relying on God, but that we are using helpful resources (as long as they do not contradict Scripture). Asking God to help you overcome your destructive thought patterns is also a helpful part of the process. It takes time and practice to shed the old ways and learn new ways to approach things. Be patient with yourself.

One thing that cognitive therapists use is called *thought stopping*. Thought stopping is simply monitoring your inner thoughts and recognizing the language or phrases you use. You can do this by asking yourself: *how am I feeling?* And, *why am I feeling this way?* Then it is important to translate your feelings into a sentence, such as: *when I am preparing for a test, I feel terrified because I feel it would be horrible if I don't get an A.* You can then start to change patterns by catching your *self-defeating thoughts* and then modifying your thoughts to be more appropriate to the situation, such as: *if I don't get an A, it will be disappointing, but not horrible.* Just changing the semantics of our extreme inner language can begin to lower our anxiety level and allow us to focus more clearly.

Another example might be when a perfectionist tells himself: *I did a horrible job,* when everyone else can see that he did a great job. (Remember, to the perfectionist, if it is not perfect, then it is horrible.) It is important to start a process of identifying your inner language and also recognizing that you are focusing on the one thing that you could have done better if only you had the time. Receiving feedback from others is also important. Many perfectionists have a hard time believing the compliments of their friends and colleagues. They dismiss the compliments, much like Wonder Woman deflected the bullets from her wrist bands. We must learn to receive compliments and feedback and to value the input from others.

This is also called *all or nothing* thinking. It occurs when we simplify by seeing things in extremes. We either did *great* or *horrible* and we fail to see anything in between. It is important to avoid swinging back and forth in such extreme thoughts. Scripture makes it clear that "the man who fears God will avoid all extremes" (Eccl. 7:18). We need to temper our thinking and be okay with our imperfections. It is an essential part of life to accept that we will never be perfect in our earthly lives. God's grace exists because of our imperfections and to meet our needs when we fail in our own efforts. It is an extension of God's love for us.

Ask yourself: *What am I telling myself? When did I start thinking this way? Is it really appropriate considering feedback I am getting from others or the level of anxiety I am experiencing? Who is demanding this standard—me, or someone else? Is it really worth this much stress? Am I allowing myself to experience God's grace in this situation?*

Then, write down some of your inner thoughts and modify them to be more balanced. Such as, *It's not perfect, but it's good enough; I am valuable even if I don't get this done perfectly; I can do a good job, but it doesn't have to be perfect;* or *Even if my house is a mess, it doesn't reflect who I am.* When we do this simple exercise, it helps us begin to change our extreme thinking and to practice more balanced thinking.

HOUSE CLUTTER

Because of my own perfectionism, I have struggled even to have friends over when my house is cluttered. This has clearly hindered my ability to enjoy some of my friendships, since my house is often cluttered. This is especially true now that I have children who create two or three messes behind every mess I clean up. Just this morning I was cleaning the Play Doh out of my hairbrush when I realized that Hannah's sippy cup was leaking red juice onto the carpeting. I went to take care of that, and then realized that I had forgotten to change the laundry load, which is what I had set out to do in the first place before I noticed the hairbrush. Then, I needed to find my kitchen utensils, which I think I saw my kids taking out to the back yard. You get the point.

I feel that I want to invest time in my kids, take them to the park, read them books, and let them play with their toys instead of watching TV. Yet, I also want to have an organized, decorated, clean house for my guests. I quickly realized that I couldn't do both perfectly without losing sleep or quality time with my friends or family. If the house was perfect, I had to neglect precious time with the kids. If I spend all of my time with my kids, doing everything I feel they need to feel loved and nurtured, the house ends up a disaster. I was forced to contend with this very real issue and make a compromise with myself. For many people this is a no brainer, just find the balance in between. But for the perfectionist, this is sheer terror! Now, I try to make sure the house is clean, but if it is a bit cluttered, or the dishes are only partially done, I don't panic and worry about what others think about me.

Forcing myself to allow people to come over when my house isn't perfect has helped me get past it. At first I would often apologize profusely to the point that my friends were annoyed with my apologies. I felt great relief when I went to friends' homes that weren't perfect. It made me feel more normal. I realized that if I wait for my house to be perfect before I invite people over, I will limit my ability to enjoy the richness of the relationships God has given me. My friends minister to me greatly when we spend time together as we chat and share struggles. I also enjoy being able to listen to their struggles and laugh with them. We need to stop looking to external sources of self-esteem, such as the perfect house, the coordinated outfit, the ideal car, and enjoy relationships and life more thoroughly. I have learned that friendships are more important than getting everything done, and finding a balance has made me happier.

The key to changing this is to struggle with your inner insecurities, and in small doses, let them be revealed. It doesn't take long to learn that the floor didn't swallow you up and the end of the world didn't come. It isn't a catastrophe. It is just a little clutter. When people reassure you that they still like spending time with you, believe it. Take in the new information and adjust. You can apply these principles to any situation where you struggle with perfectionistic tendencies. Ask God to reveal them to you and to help you find a healthier balance. You will find that you will begin to relax and enjoy things more.

THE BEAUTY IS IN THE IMPERFECTION

When I was planning my wedding, I was still struggling with perfectionism. I had made some progress but was still demanding excessive standards for myself. A wedding to plan and a perfectionist to plan it is not a good combination! It is a recipe for stress. I was feeling very compulsive about planning each detail, and every spare moment I had I tended to obsess about the wedding planning. What about the dresses? The programs have to be just so. What about the cake? What if the DJ plays a bad song? I fretted. As we got closer, I started to feel weary from the details and recognized that I hadn't made as much progress as I thought on letting go of my perfectionistic tendencies. My self-esteem was still partially wrapped up in getting the details right for the big day.

God spoke to me in the middle of my full-blown neurotic need to perfect my wedding plans by gently telling me a phrase I would hold onto. He said to me, "The beauty is in the imperfection." I pondered it and tried to hold onto it. It became my mantra when things didn't go as planned. I shared with a friend of mine God's word for me, and she smiled and said I sounded like a "desperate perfectionist." And it was true, I *was* a desperate perfectionist. Desperate for a way to calm my need to have everything just so, to be accepted the way I am. I needed a way to cope with the fact that in real life things change and don't go just as planned, no matter how much effort we put into the planning.

The wedding was beautiful, and I was able to enjoy it entirely, even though several things didn't go exactly the way I had planned. I remembered what God had told me, and with His help, I was able to believe it and focus on what was really important. Just as the markings on a butterfly aren't perfectly symmetrical, our life is often marked by asymmetry. There is beauty in that fact. Flowers even have a bit of imperfection on each bloom, and they are all beautifully created. Similarly, our lives are marked by imperfection, and often things do not go as planned. We need to let go of our strivings to make things perfect by our own will and effort. God's love and grace are there to meet us, and He loves our imperfections and desires to befriend us.

IMPERFECT PROCESS

I have spent the most time on this chapter because I feel that it is a critical point to grasp. When people start trying to work on self-improvement, it can often be a process that just highlights what we are failing at, and our sense of inadequacy surfaces. Spiritual growth is an imperfect process, and we will stumble and make mistakes. Embracing this process as an imperfect one will help. This side of heaven we will always fall short. That is why we need God's infinite grace in our lives to help us grow and flourish.

POINTS TO CONSIDER: PERFECTIONISM VS. TRUST

- Perfectionism is rooted in insecurity and in all-or-nothing thinking.
- Perfectionism is reliance on our own strivings instead of on God's grace. God's grace fills in the gaps as we rely on Him.
- God's grace is sufficient for us, and there is beauty in the imperfections in our lives.

EXPLORATION QUESTIONS

1. Am I sometimes a perfectionist? In what areas?
2. What drives my perfectionism?
3. How can I learn to experience God's grace for me?
4. How can I trust God more in these areas?

FOCUS VERSE

"My grace is sufficient for you, for my power is made perfect in weakness." Therefore I will boast all the more gladly about my weaknesses, so that Christ's power may rest on me. That is why, for Christ's sake, I delight in weaknesses, in insults, in hardships, in persecutions, in difficulties. For when I am weak, then I am strong.

—2 Corinthians 12:9–10

FOCUS PRAYER

Lord, forgive me for trying to be what only You can be— perfect. Thank You that you take the burden off of me to be perfect. Help me to step back and allow Your grace to fill my life. May I seek You in my weaknesses rather than rely on my own efforts. Forgive me for denying Your grace and not trusting that You have everything I need. I trust You, Lord. In Jesus' name, amen.

CHAPTER 3

THE WEED OF WORRY VS. THE FRUIT OF PEACE

ANTICIPATORY ANXIETY

ANTICIPATING THE WORST, a worrier expects negative outcomes and often feels tremendously uneasy. This unease includes an inability to rest in one's mind and spirit. Cognitive-Behavioral Therapists call this *Anticipatory Anxiety*—when we anticipate the worst outcome and fret about it, whether it has happened or not. Just the thought that it *could* happen raises anxiety, and worriers will have difficulty convincing themselves that it is not worth stressing about. Indeed, worrying creates a great deal of anxiety and stress, much of which is unnecessary.

THE FUTILITY OF WORRY

Of course, the enemy would love to have us focus on the worst possible outcome and spend our precious time preoccupied with it. Possibly this is why the gospels urge us to put aside worry by inquiring, "Who of you by worrying can add a single hour to his life? Since you cannot do this very little thing, why do you worry about the rest?" (Luke 12:25–26). This verse emphasizes the futility of worry. The gospel writer asks a searching question to cause us to evaluate our own thoughts. We are faced with a choice: waste our time with worry or have peace in our hearts that God can handle our deepest struggles.

FEAR AND MISTRUST

Worry is rooted in fear and mistrust. When we fear the worst without any evidence of it actually taking place, we are allowing fear to rule our thoughts, which will inevitably influence our actions. It is also an active mistrust of God, often placed on Him as a projection of what our past has dictated. Possibly we grew up in an unpredictable home, or we have been sorely disappointed. Many of us have been betrayed by those we put our trust in. Situations where we hoped for a positive outcome turned sour, leaving our hearts sagging in the aftermath. We begin to generalize our past hurts and project them into the future and onto God. We convince ourselves that He doesn't care about us, and we abandon our faith and trust for an attitude that we need to fend for ourselves. Our hearts are filled with fear.

Some of us have suffered great pain and losses. Even watching the evening news raises fear in our hearts of what has happened to some, and we start to feel uneasy. It is very apparent that life is full of hardships that we'd like to steer clear of as much as we can. Even as believers with great faith, we need to be vigilant and do our part to be safe. Letting go of worry doesn't mean that we live carelessly or recklessly. We must take the general precautions and keep in mind that the enemy is like a "roaring lion looking for someone to devour" (1 Pet. 5:8).

However, let us not blame the enemy's work on our loving God and Friend. It is important to keep in mind that

God can turn any evil into a chance for spiritual rebirth and growth. Take great comfort in knowing that "in all things God works for the good of those who love Him, who have been called according to His purpose" (Rom. 8:28). We are assured that God will bring to justice those who wrong us (Luke 18:8) and will bring forth fruit from what the enemy does that is intended to harm us. I have experienced fruit and growth during the times it seemed that all was working against me.

CHRONIC WORRY

Personally, I have experienced some types of events that can lead to chronic worry and fear. I have twice been approached by attackers. In both situations my life was at stake, and God intervened to insure that I would survive. I was quite shaken and even injured, but in the end, I was safe and spared from death. I look back on each one and can see that God used what the enemy intended for evil to bring me to a greater depth of understanding of Him and of what He was leading me toward in my life.

I have had to struggle with anticipating the worst, especially since I have experienced some traumatic situations. Yet, I choose to walk in faith that God is in control and to trust in His loving care. When I begin to worry, I choose to turn my thoughts into a prayer and cry out to God for help and for peace. When we are in a place where we struggle to grasp circumstances fully, we need to pray in the way that the centurion prayed when he said, "I do believe; help me overcome my unbelief!" (Mark 9:24).

"TAKE HEART"

We are not guaranteed perfect safety at all times. Terrible things do happen—even to believers, yet we need to trust that God will bring us through it and provide for all of our needs. Jesus confirms that we are not free from problems. "I have told you these things, so *that in me you may have peace. In this world you will have trouble. But take heart! I have overcome the world!*" (John 16:33, emphasis added). This truth helps us focus on eternal things and recognize that our sufferings are only temporary (2 Cor. 4:18).

When we allow fear and mistrust to dictate our spiritual lives practically and fundamentally, our relationship with God suffers. Indeed we suffer from the effects of our own worry. The worrier's inner life is often filled with *what ifs—What if I let others down...that would be horrible. What if I am perceived as a failure? What if they don't like my work? What will others think of me?* We tell ourselves that such things would be *awful* and *horrible.*

COGNITIVE CHANGES

Worriers tend to treat a wide range of situations with fear fueled by our inner language. The cognitive theorist Albert Ellis calls these *Automatic Thoughts*, because we tend to think them so frequently and quickly that we aren't even aware we are doing it. The extreme, anxiety producing thoughts are so ingrained in our inner thought life that they are automatic. One thing we can do to shift away from unnecessary worry is to catch ourselves using the strong words *horrible, awful,* or whatever words you use, and then modify our wording to more moderate language such as: *that would be disappointing or uncomfortable.* It is important that we don't treat everything as a crisis or as *the end of the world.* Ellis would call this *catastrophising.* Let's reserve our strong emotional reactions for things that really require it, rather than for benign situations that are really just disappointments and not catastrophes.

UNEXPECTED SITUATIONS

I remember a story one of my pastors told me that when they had invited guests over during the winter, they had prepared a casserole beforehand for their guests and set it out on the back porch to cool. When their guests arrived, and it was time to eat, they went out to get the casserole. Much to their dismay, the dish was empty, and apparently cleaned as if there never had been a casserole. Wondering what had happened, they looked around and noticed their sweet Labrador had also been outside, and was now contentedly licking her lips and looking for a nice spot to take a nap. They had forgotten she was outside.

If you were in this situation, I ask, would you be able to laugh about it with your guests, or would you panic and believe it to be a catastrophe? Would you worry about what your guests thought about you? Would you convince yourself that it was horrible that you failed to provide them with a home-cooked meal, or would you accept your disappointment and figure out from where you might order in?

I admit there was a time in my life that I would have seen this as a total catastrophe. I would have been horrified and ashamed. I would have needed lots of reassurance. Thankfully, I think I would cope with it better now. I have worked hard at shifting my inner thoughts and have reserved the words *horrible* or *awful* for things that really deserve it. It doesn't always come easily, but if I work at it, I can do it.

GOD'S COMFORT

We all worry about things from time to time. It is natural to have concerns, and it is important to be realistic about life's challenges. However, if we allow our fears to invade our daily thought life, we are robbed of enjoyment and freedom from fear. It is the enemy's goal to rob us of things that God has given us. One of the things he wants to rob us of is peace of mind. Worry and peace really are incompatible. God comforts us and assures us that peace comes from Him and that we can possess it even in the midst of awful circumstances. "Do not be anxious about anything, but in everything, by prayer and petition, with thanksgiving, present your requests to God. And the peace of God, which transcends all understanding, will guard your hearts and your minds in Christ Jesus" (Phil. 4:7). His peace guards us and surrounds us, even in the darkest of times.

There are times in our lives when anyone would be confounded by our peace, but God gives it to us in an eternal perspective, and it is wrapped in His love for us. We know that even when things on earth go wrong, we will be with Him one day, free from the pain we endure on Earth. "Therefore we do not lose heart. Though outwardly we are wasting away, yet inwardly we are being renewed day by day. For our light and momentary troubles are achieving for us an eternal glory that far outweighs them all. So we fix our eyes not on what is seen, but on what is unseen. For what is seen is temporary, but what is unseen is eternal" (2 Cor. 4:16–18).

The most important thing to do when wrestling with the problem of worry in our lives is to explore what Scripture says about worry:

> Therefore I tell you, do not worry about your life, what you will eat or drink; or about your body, what you will wear. Is not life more important than food, and the body more important than clothes? Look at the birds of the air; they do not sow or reap or store away in barns, and

yet your heavenly Father feeds them. Are you not much more valuable than they?

—Matthew 6:25–26

We are of great value to God, and He promises to take care of us. Recognizing our value to Him soothes the worry wart inside of us. When we worry we need to remember how much God cares about us.

EACH DAY HAS TROUBLE

God is clear with us that worrying is a waste of time. It takes away from us precious time and indicates a profound distrust in God's sovereignty and love for us. It also hinders us from focusing on what we need to address in the present moment, because we are preoccupied:

And why do you worry about clothes? See how the lilies of the field grow. They do not labor or spin. Yet I tell you that not even Solomon in all his splendor was dressed like one of these. If that is how God clothes the grass of the field, which is here today and tomorrow is thrown into the fire, will he not much more clothe you, O you of little faith? So do not worry, saying, "What shall we eat?" or "What shall we drink?" or "What shall we wear?" For the pagans run after all these things, and your heavenly Father knows that you need them. But seek first his kingdom and his righteousness, and all these things will be given to you as well. *Therefore do not worry about tomorrow, for tomorrow will worry about itself. Each day has enough trouble of its own.*

—Matthew 6:28–34, emphasis mine

Isn't that true? Each day does have trouble. If we are overly focused on the uncertainty of our future, then we

35

are often paralyzed from being able to focus our time and energy on what we need to be doing in the present. We tend not only to worry about the practical things, whether we will have what we need or hope for, but also we worry about impractical things in today's society. We worry about status, degrees, fashion, technology, the "next best thing." We get caught up in the unimportant and forget about what truly is important.

REAL RELATIONSHIP

We lose sight of relationship with God and with others. We worry about what others think about us, but fail to be concerned with how we can help one another. I see young girls striving for appearance and attractiveness, when underneath they feel insecure and uncertain. Worrying about superficial things damages true relationship. We worry that our house is just so, our clothes updated, we want our car to be current, and we strive to impress others. When we worry about such things, true relationship cannot occur, because these things are exterior and not matters of the heart.

This happens at church as well. We want to appear that we have it all together. We wear a smile on our face, dress for church, and are pleasant to those we say hello to, because we are concerned about our image. We think that if we appear to be composed and go through the motions of church, we will maintain the image that we have it all together. We worry that we won't be able to maintain that image, and when others start to see that we are struggling, hurting, or learning from our mistakes, we feel embarrassed.

Wouldn't it be better to be concerned about more substantial things? Authenticity is important in relationships. When we move away from concerning ourselves with superficiality, we can begin to have authentic relationships. When we have authentic relationships, we minister to one another, listen to one another, and get to know what makes others happy or sad and what interests they have. Then we can appreciate differences and care for one another when we are hurting. We can pray for our neighbor, intercede for our friend, and minister to the poor, because we recognize that we are not the only one with things to worry about. Helping others helps us worry less about our self and gives us a bigger perspective on what really is important.

I am not saying that you should feel guilty if you get a new outfit that you like. It is okay to enjoy things we have, but we need to worry less about how we look and more about caring for others. God has a habit of providing for those who minister to others. When we think less about ourselves, we allow the Holy Spirit to move in our lives.

HOPE FOR THE WORRIER

Instead of asking "what if?" it is important to start telling yourself, *It is going to be okay. God is in control.* Ask yourself, *How do I know that X is going to happen, it might not...therefore, I refuse to worry until I know how it has turned out, until then I will assume it is okay.* For example, I used to panic whenever I could not find my purse. My heart would start racing and I would start a frantic search for it. Once I found it, I would have to calm down from my panic, which I now realize was completely unnecessary stress since the purse was nearby all along.

Now I choose to stay calm when I can't locate my purse, and I choose not to panic until I have looked everywhere. I realize also that if indeed I can't find my purse, it will be a hassle to cancel bank cards, but it really is not the end of the world since I am okay and my loved ones are okay.

OUR LOVED ONES

I realize that worriers tend to worry a great deal about their loved ones. When they haven't heard from a son, daughter, spouse, or other loved one, the anxiety immediately begins to rise, and worriers go to town fretting and may even feel slightly ill. Soon, thereafter, their loved ones call or drive up the driveway having been fine all along. They tend to look at their worried parent, spouse, or loved one with puzzlement when they hear just how worried they have been.

When I was home for a visit from college, I remember distinctly a time my mom had panicked when I came home later than expected. I was accustomed to the freedom of college life, and it hadn't occurred to me to call her to let her know where I was. We didn't have cell phones yet, and when I walked in, I found her waiting for me on the couch, beside herself with worry. Moments later some friends drove up whom she had called, and they had gone out looking for me. I was wide-eyed with wonder about why everyone was so worried about me. I had just lost track of time talking with my childhood friend I hadn't seen in months. Now, as a parent, I do understand the fear that parents experience in regards to their children's well-being. We feel tremendous fear about what might happen to those we love.

TIME CONSUMING

What I have found is that chronic worriers tend to worry both about the big things and the small things. How time consuming is this worry! It penetrates the mind and soul and consumes the worrier. Most often there really is not much to worry about, since everyone is fine and disaster is not impending. Why then do I give the purse example? I give the purse example because in learning to let go of worry we need to start small. Once I began to let go of worry about my missing purse, I realized I could then transfer what I had learned to other worrisome moments in my life, and the more I practiced, the more I was able to release my worry.

Worriers need lots of inner reassurance, and they have trouble holding reassurance within themselves. Telling ones self, *I will get through this okay,* or *If it doesn't go well, it will be okay,* doesn't compute emotionally. Often worriers have experienced a stressful or traumatic outcome in the past, so their body remembers and anticipates the worst, or they may have had parents who were worriers and learned this behavior from them. In addition, we are bombarded by news media coverage of tragic and terrible events all of the time. If you are a worrier by nature, and you find that watching the news adds fuel to the worry wart in you, then I strongly suggest you reduce your viewing of the news.

THE PEACE OF GOD

Philippians 4:7–8 says, "And the peace of God, which transcends all understanding, will guard your hearts and your minds in Christ Jesus." What we need to understand is that peace in our hearts opposes worry. It indicates trust in a loving God who can make all things good in His time. Yes, there are things to worry about. Yet chronic worry shows a lack of faith in God. "We know that in all things God works for the good of those who love him, who have been called according to his purpose" (Rom. 8:28). We have reassurance that provides peace.

When I begin to worry, and we all worry from time to time, I try to catch myself and begin to turn my worry into prayer. It is important to confess our lack of trust and submit to God by praying for whomever or whatever it is we are worrying about. It is in those moments that we can experience the "peace of God that transcends all understanding" (Phil. 4:7). It is difficult to understand why anyone would feel at peace when so much can go wrong and when we see and experience pain all around us. Often, even in the midst of a painful situation, I hear believers say, "I feel a peace inside." That is the Holy Spirit indwelling our hearts and comforting us when nothing makes sense and when life is challenging. God is in control and loves us deeply. It is on that truth we must stand and surrender our worries to Him.

God asks us to focus instead on "whatever is true, whatever is noble, whatever is right, whatever is pure, whatever is lovely, whatever is admirable—if anything is excellent or praiseworthy—think about such things. Whatever you have learned or received or heard from me, or seen in me—put it into practice. And the God of peace will be with you" (Phil. 4:8–9). We must choose to focus on what is positive and be thankful in our hearts rather than focus on the negative or the *potential* for negative. The enemy would be delighted to bind us up in our worries and hold us back from enjoying the blessings and love of God when we surrender our worries to Him.

SURRENDER WORRY

When we surrender our worries to God in prayer, we allow Him to intervene, we express trust in Him, and we make room for peace to enter our uneasy hearts. If our hearts and mind are troubled by worry, then there isn't any spare room for peace. It gets choked out or pushed aside. The very thought of it evades us, and worry takes root deeper and deeper in our hearts. It becomes habitual. On the contrary, if we choose to seek God's presence in our restless hearts that are prone to worry, then we get a chance to experience the peace that transcends understanding (Phil. 4:7). Sometimes this is a daily choice we make or even a moment by moment choice. We must choose to refrain from allowing worry to reside in our hearts. We must turn our circumstances over to God. This is where my love for the serenity prayer surfaces:

> God grant me the serenity to accept the things I cannot change, the courage to change the things I can, and the wisdom to know the difference.
>
> The Serenity Prayer by Reinhold Neibuhr

This prayer is so beautiful in its simplicity and is something that has blessed me deeply. During the years that I facilitated a heroin addicts' recovery group, we would stand hand in hand saying this prayer at the end of group. We did this for three years, and I felt it changing me. I could see a difference in myself that was tangible. I had more insight and was truly able to accept the things that I couldn't change. If you have not yet made this prayer a part of your life, please do. Post it on your mirror and recite it in the morning while you brush your teeth or comb your hair. Over time, it will make an impact.

In conclusion, worry robs us of enjoying life's blessings and takes the fun out of our days. Rather than holding on to the habit of worry, release your worries to God with the knowledge that He loves you more than anything else He has created. You have the capacity for relationship with Him, and it is His desire to care for you. It doesn't make our life free of stress and hardships, but it comforts us during our trials and gives us hope that He will carry us through whatever we face in this lifetime.

POINTS TO CONSIDER: WORRY VS. PEACE

- Worry is futile and wastes time.
- The peace of God counters unnecessary worry and calms our hearts.
- We can choose to focus on hope and trust in God rather than worry about things needlessly.

EXPLORATION QUESTIONS

1. Do I worry? What do I worry about?
2. What drives my worry?
3. How can I seek God's peace and loving care?
4. How can I surrender my worry to God?
5. How can I accept the things I cannot change?

FOCUS VERSE

Therefore I tell you, do not worry about your life, what you will eat or drink; or about your body, what you will wear. Is not life more important than food, and the body more important than clothes? Look at the birds of the air; they do not sow or reap or store away in barns, and yet your heavenly Father feeds them. Are you not much more valuable than they? Who of you by worrying can add a single hour to his life?

—Matthew 6:25–27

FOCUS PRAYER

Lord, I know that I am prone to worry. You know my anxieties. Help me to learn to trust You more and to surrender my worries to You so that I can experience Your peace that goes beyond understanding. I know that You are trustworthy and can help me through whatever it is that I face in this life. Thank You for helping me every day, help me to live in the present and not to fear the future. In Jesus' name, amen.

CHAPTER 4

THE WEED OF VICTIMHOOD VS.
THE FRUIT OF CONFIDENCE

WHEN WE EXPERIENCE defeat, feel chronically frustrated, or lose hope, our human nature naturally declares we are victims. We begin to speak to ourselves negatively. We tell ourselves we are hopeless, dumb, unappreciated, and failures. Sometimes our inner language is mildly critical, and for others of us, it is a bigger criticism. In the land of victimhood there are self-critics and all-out victims.

Self-critics will put themselves down and focus on their weaknesses. They tend to see the empty portion of the glass and see it as a reflection of themselves. Critics beat up on themselves often through harsh and critical self-talk. Sometimes this inner criticism is hidden from others within one's own thought life. For others, everyone around is fully aware of the negative thought life of critics. They will express out loud: "I'm so fat." "That was stupid." Or, "I should have done better." Self-critics constantly put themselves down. It may become so natural that the thoughts become habitual.

Victims are much harder on themselves than self-critics. They will speak to themselves in self-depreciating statements that lead to feelings of hopelessness. Whereas critics can still feel good about themselves at times, the victim feels poorly about themselves and views their faults as a never-ending pattern of defeat. Their negative inner language goes something like this: *I'll never be good at anything. I'm just a burden to everybody. I always screw things up. Why bother? Everybody hates me. I never do it right.* You can see how debilitating this inner language is to the individual with a victim mindset.

Just as if we had victim sunglasses on, everything we see and experience comes through that lens. Instead of UVA or UVB rays being blocked out, anything positive or hopeful about ourselves or our situation gets blocked out, and we can't see it. Once we stop seeing the positive, we only take in information that proves we are what we believe we are—victims.

THE SOURCE

Many of us with a victim's mindset have indeed been victimized at one time in our life or perhaps even repetitively. We might, in fact, be suffering adversity and be a victim of negative circumstances, abuse, hopelessness, job loss, or other adverse conditions. When we experience constant frustration in our attempts to survive our circumstances, we can develop what counselors call *learned helplessness*. If our abusers made us feel helpless by what they said to us or how they treated us, then we learn that we are helpless to overcome our circumstances.

Possibly, we received strong negative feedback in the form of verbal abuse. "You will never amount to anything." Or, "You are just like your father." Or worse, "I wish you were never born!" Or you might hear similar, but mild, disappointment. "That's not good enough. Why can't you be more like your sister?" These are words that whack away at our self-esteem and confidence.

Others of us have been beaten down by life. Maybe you couldn't afford college, and now finding a job that provides for you and your family evades you. Possibly you were laid off from your job, and finding a new one has been hard. Perhaps you grew up where schools were poorly funded, and you decided to skip out on school because it was boring and you felt you were never given a chance to succeed. Perhaps you have experienced multiple losses, or have gone through a divorce. Maybe you have lost your home, or worse, a beloved family member. Life itself may bring challenges and hurts that can leave us feeling victimized.

Sometimes we feel like a victim because we were spoiled as a child. Our parents gave us everything we wanted when we wanted it. Life was smooth and easy for us because someone always picked up after us, or we never got a sense of what it was like to struggle for something. Then real life happened, and you started to experience the fact that life is not that easy. We feel victimized by the fact that life is hard, because we weren't given a realistic impression of it as a child. We weren't properly prepared for life's challenges.

CHANGING THE VICTIM MINDSET

Believing that we are victims comes in many different varieties. We might think we are unlikable, ugly, dumb, or that we are always going to fail. When I was younger, I was plagued by these thoughts. I felt terrible about myself, and my actions reflected it. I didn't apply myself in high school because I felt I was dumb. I thought I was ugly, and I sometimes even would say that I hated myself. It was a dark time in my life, and I struggled to pull out of the darkness. I gradually was able to pull myself out of this mindset with God's help.

Part of the work was taking in new information that I refused to see. I had to learn that people did like me, that I wasn't ugly (no one is), and that I could make good friends and do well in school. It involved taking risks and knowing how much God loves me. Scripture even acknowledges how our hearts turn against us. "This, then, is how we know that we belong to the truth and how we set our hearts at rest in His presence *whenever our hearts condemn us.* For God is greater than our hearts and He knows everything" (see 1 John 3:19, emphasis mine).

Recovery involves placing our hearts in His hands where He can heal us, since our own hearts tend to "condemn" us. Sometimes we confuse our own condemning thoughts with God's and aren't able to understand that God desires to extend grace (His favor) on us.

When we trust Him with our self-condemning thoughts and confide in Him, we learn that is not how He feels about us. We begin to experience His love and acceptance by the power of the Holy Spirit in our hearts. King David expressed his discovery of God's love in the Psalms, "Praise is to the LORD, for he showed His wonderful love to me" (Ps. 31:21).

INNER DIALOGUE

Notice also that the victim tends to use the words *always* and *never* in reference to themselves or their circumstances. For example, if something goes wrong, the victim will proclaim, "I always screw that up." Or they will say, "It never goes right for me." It is a common and destructive habit to get into. One of the first steps is to catch yourself using polarizing words that give no room for grace. We need to learn to receive God's grace for us so that we can also learn to give grace to ourselves when we mess up. "In him we have redemption through his blood, the forgiveness of sins, in accordance with the riches of God's grace that he lavished on us with all wisdom and understanding" (Eph. 1:7–8).

We must begin to temper our inner language and remove the words *always* and *never* and replace them with *often* or *sometimes*. For example, change your inner dialogue deliberately to: *I sometimes mess up, but it's okay. It's not horrible.* Subtle changes are important, because we need to recognize our strengths. Even if we don't believe it at first, once we start to change our inner language, our emotions will catch up eventually, and we will feel more hopeful.

CRUEL WORDS

Sometimes we think these things in response to others' cruel words toward us. Some of us have heard harsh words from critical parents or heard cruel things said on the playground at school. We often take these things to heart, and they stick around and make a home in our hearts. Once we believe the negative words, whether they are true or not, we begin to feel defeated. For some it is a minor problem, and for others these negative labels consume their thought life and their feelings about themselves. How deeply it affects you often depends on early life experiences and the frequency and severity of the negative or harsh words said.

Sometimes these messages come from neglect instead. When parents are too busy for their children, whether they are wealthy or not, the children recognize the actions have meaning linked to them…that we are not worth their time or investment. This message will be internalized.

DIVORCE

Granted, it gets harder and harder for modern day parents to insure that kids are invested in by their primary attachment figures. The need to make ends meet often requires dual income, and it is tough for parents to spend the time kids need to feel valued and loved. The challenges of divorced families also add multiple issues. That is why it is critical to either make some financial sacrifices or make a point of verbalizing to your kids how much they are loved and valued, and that you wish you were able to go to every sports game, school play, or event. When you are at home, take time to eat meals together, play games together, and ask your kids how their day was. If you cannot be there, make time for a phone call. These things all communicate to kids that they are valued and loved.

Even though my parents divorced and lived three hours apart, I was aware that I was valued. My dad worked a 40-hour work week in four days so that he could drive three hours up to Michigan to visit with me for three day weekends. It was a sacrifice of time, but one I am glad he consistently chose to make, because his visits made me feel wanted. Many parents disappear after divorce, hardly seeing their kids at all. Even though he wasn't able to go to track events or other things because it was impractical, the consistent effort made a big difference in my life and created positive memories that I hold onto.

If you are divorced, find creative ways to communicate to your kids that you care about them. It will make a big difference. If your parents were divorced and you were shuffled around as a result, it is important to understand that Jesus will never shuffle you around. He always cares for you and is always there for you. Parents are imperfect and life is often unfair, we must forgive our parents for their shortcomings and not let their shortcomings define us. We may have been victims of life's challenges at one time, but with God's help, we can rise above our circumstances.

OUR OWN ACTIONS

Sometimes, when we already feel poorly about ourselves, it will affect how we respond to others. This will reinforce what we already believe about ourselves. If we think we are unlikable or uninteresting, we will approach a social gathering with our head down, eyes to the floor, and a hesitancy to engage with others. Then, when we leave the party feeling rejected, we may fail to see how our own actions contributed to the way others responded to us. Others may simply respect what you communicate through your actions and leave you alone. Often people may not want to work extra hard to make sure you are comfortable. Relationships are developed when two people equally engage in the process of getting to know each other and invest in the relationship.

Those of us with a victim mindset are very sensitive to rejection and may interpret the lack of interest from others as proof we are unlikable. However, we must understand that not everyone we meet will be able to invest in us as friends. People are limited to time constraints that only make it possible to be actively invested in a few friendships at one time. This is also known as *generalizing* when we experience rejection and assume that it will be an ongoing pattern of defeat. Depending on how strong our victim mindset is, we will give up easily, because we already assume that because one person wasn't interested, then no one will be. We give up before we give others a chance.

How We Approach God

This attitude can also affect our relationship with God. We approach Him the same way. We think He doesn't like us, isn't interested in us, or has it out for us, just like everybody else. When we feel this way, based on our assumptions, we either approach God with hesitancy and reluctance or refuse to approach Him at all. We generalize from our human experiences and project our pain onto God, assuming He will *be a jerk, just like my uncle who abused me,* or *He will just tell me I don't measure up, and I already know that, so I don't need to hear it from God.* We assume the negative and aren't able to see the truth that God loves us very dearly.

The reality is that God is always interested in you and eager to engage in conversation and relationship with you. However, He is a perfect gentleman. He won't force you or push a relationship with you. He waits for your response to Him. "Behold I stand at the door and knock" (Rev. 3:20). Just as at a party most people won't spend time begging you to engage with them if you are unwilling, Jesus will patiently wait for you to express interest in Him, because He is very interested in you, but He does not impose: "Draw near to God and He will draw near to you" (James 4:8 KJV). He is attentively waiting for us to move closer to Him, and in response, He comes closer to us. The Lord promises that if you "seek (Him) you will find (Him)" (Matt. 7:7). Unlike people, God is not bound by time. He is guaranteed to have the time and interest to invest in your friendship if you allow Him to.

FAULTY EMOTIONAL REASONING

Another thing we tend to do when we are in a victim mindset is to use our emotions to make conclusions, also called *emotional reasoning.* We may feel rejected or hopeless. It is important to understand and to be aware of our God-given emotions. However, our emotions do not equal the truth.

Our emotions tell us important things, and when we are aware of them, we are able to use them to understand ourselves more. We learn what upsets us, what interests us, and what makes us feel sad. However, when we become caught up in emotions, we tend to *personalize* what people say or do or don't do when it may have nothing to do with us. This might happen when a spouse comes home after work and is grumpy from having a bad day. The husband or wife may assume that it is something they did and ask, "What did I do wrong?" when in fact it has only to do with a hard day at work. We all do this sometimes, but when we are in a victim mindset, we tend to take most things personally and have a hard time believing others when they try to reassure us that it has nothing to do with us.

We must be very cautious about using emotions to reason. Emotions can rapidly change and may not be based on truth or fact at all. We can take note of our emotions, but not allow them to rule our decisions or perspectives. If we feel ashamed, it is important to recognize that just because we *feel* shameful does not mean we *are* shameful. "In you I trust, O my God, do not let me be put to shame, nor let my enemies triumph over me. *No one whose hope is in you will ever be put to shame*" (Ps. 25:2–3, emphasis mine). God promises that when we place our confidence in Him, He will not shame us. We might shame ourselves, and others may have shamed us, but God will never shame us. Isn't that a relief to know—that the God of the Universe will not shame us?

We must distinguish the source of the shame as separate from God, because it is not God who shames us. It is often our own mindset which cannot be trusted. "Surely the mind and heart of man are cunning" (Ps. 64:6). Our own thoughts condemn us. On the other hand God says, "Let us then approach the throne of grace with confidence, so that we may receive mercy and find grace to help us in our time of need" (Heb. 4:16). God says that we can draw near His throne of grace, not wallowing in shame, but with our head held high in confidence that He loves us. In doing so, we receive His help.

THE THRONE OF GRACE

I was recently drawn to the story of Esther in the Old Testament. She knew that when she approached the king's throne having not been summoned, it could result in her death, since that was breaking the law of the land. Through fasting, Esther was confident enough in the king's love for her, and she took the risk of approaching his throne with a request. The king reached out his scepter to her. She touched it. This was an indication that she had found favor from him and was allowed to speak. This is an image of our relationship with God. In reverence and awe we know that he has great power and authority over us, yet we are to be confident in approaching His throne because He loves us. He loves it when we approach Him. He will gladly extend his grace to us so we can speak in confidence in His presence and not in shame.

Part of the reason the Lord wants us to *approach his throne of grace* is noted by Charles Spurgeon in his book *All of Grace*. He states, "The Lord knows very well that you cannot change your own heart and cannot cleanse your own nature. But, He also knows that He can do both." He knows that only He has the power and authority to cleanse and heal you, therefore, He never shames you.

You are not able to transform yourself, and He does not expect you to because you are "being transformed into his likeness with ever-increasing glory, which comes from the Lord, who is the Spirit" (2 Cor. 3:18). The only thing He requires is for you to allow Him to do the work—much like a baby allows their parents to change their diapers. We don't get mad at a baby because he cannot control his bowels. We know he is not able, and so we lovingly take care of him. When my daughter (who is not yet potty trained at one and a half) needs to be changed, she comes to me and says, "poo poo," which signals me to change her. I do it immediately and with pleasure. When we have fallen back into sin, we don't need to shamefully hide it. We need to come to the Lord and ask for His help, which He gladly extends to us. "So we say with confidence, The Lord is my helper; I will not be afraid" (Heb. 13:6). It is the enemy who tells us that we ought to be ashamed and who attempts to keep us isolated in our shame, unable to ask for help. Pride and shame often work together. When we are too prideful to admit that we have made a mistake, it is partly because we are ashamed of it.

JESUS, MAN OF SORROWS

"He was despised and rejected by men, a man of sorrows, and familiar with suffering. Like one from whom men hide their faces he was despised, and we esteemed him not. Surely he took up our infirmities and carried our sorrows" (Isa. 53:3–4).

In His own suffering, Jesus not only took upon Himself the punishment that our sins deserve but also became a man who knows our grief firsthand. This was intentional so that, "According to his eternal purpose which he accomplished in Christ Jesus our Lord. In him and through faith in him we may approach God with freedom and confidence." (Eph. 3:11–12). Because Jesus suffered for us, we can come to the Lord in confidence. He bore our shame. He was rejected. He was abandoned for our glory! So that we can one day be glorified with Him in the heavens and ensured that we are not abandoned.

Who are we to proclaim that we are the victim and wallow in it when Jesus paid such a great, personal price to overcome a victim mindset for us? Wallowing in it is a way of rejecting Jesus' sacrifice on the Cross. We must not wallow in our shame or take pride in it. We must instead look to Him to carry us through our pain, knowing full well that He is a man who can fully comprehend what we are going through and can take us through it.

GREENER PASTURES

In the devotional *A Shepherd Looks at Psalm 23* by Phillip Keller, we learn that shepherds are always scouting out greener pastures for their sheep, and they guide the sheep there. It is necessary for them to be led to the new pasture by the shepherd because "sheep are notorious creatures of habit. If left to themselves they will follow the same trails until they become ruts; graze the same hills until they turn into desert wastes; pollute their own ground until it is corrupt with disease and parasites." We are prone to stay in our own ruts, and we are unable to find the way out unless we are led out by our spiritual shepherd, Jesus. He knows the way to greener pastures, free of weeds and parasites, and knows how to lead us there. We must be willing to follow and trust Him, or we will be the victim of our own choice to stay back where we feel hopeless yet attracted to the familiarity of victim-hood.

If we are being victimized or abused we must look to God to help us to find our way out. "This is the assurance we have in approaching God: that if we ask anything according to his will, he hears us" (1 John 5:14). We must pray for God to carry us through and to give us the strength we need and to show us where to go. Our prayers do not fall on empty ears. He will answer us.

THE PROBLEM OF PRIDE

Some of us are not really being victimized, but we feel like victims. Every time something doesn't go our way, we feel life is unfair. This is where pride comes in, because sometimes we just don't want to change our ways. Attracted to the lure of *secondary gain,* we hold onto our victim mindset. We use our victim mentality to draw attention from others who may extend sympathy toward us. Possibly we are able to use it to manipulate others to feel bad for us, or to feel guilty that they aren't doing enough to appease us. Unable to see how this is affecting us negatively, we linger in the victim rut.

There was a particular morning that I awoke in an unshakable grouchy mood. I was feeling sorry for myself and focusing on the negative. I attempted to talk myself through it, but I couldn't seem to get past it. I brought my negative mood to God. I told Him how badly I didn't want to go to work and how awful I was feeling and that I was going to need help getting out of this dreadful mood I was in. Interestingly, I found myself switching shirts from a white button down to a dark green wool sweater and started off for work with a friend. I was completing an internship in Philadelphia at the time, and we walked to the EL train for work.

That day it had been raining. I hadn't noticed that everyone else had stayed back from the curb as I confidently walked right up to the edge, and sploosh! I was hit with a tidal wave of puddle water from the street as a car drove by. It splashed right into my face like a giant wave, and it soaked me completely. Standing there sopping wet with my styled hair flattened and hairspray running down my face, I started laughing hysterically. Immediately my mood was transformed, and I stopped taking life so seriously. I thought, *God you are funny!* I knew that was how He had answered my prayer to help me out of my mood. To the amazement of everyone around me, I just laughed the rest of the way to work and had a great day. Sometimes, it is important to lighten up and stop taking things so seriously.

Some of us have a hard time shifting gears when life starts to go more positively. We hold onto our bad mood and scowl. Improvements challenge us, and we don't know how to be when we are doing better.

If things start to go well in our life, we might not be aware that we are deeply uncomfortable with it because that fact challenges our victim mindset. As a result, we may create conflict or sabotage our progress. We do this because we are not ready or willing to let go of secondary gain and take a hold of *primary gain* where we can feel good about ourselves and our successes, and regain confidence in more positive ways. When we are so used to being a victim, we feel challenged and frightened of successes. At least we know what to expect when we are the victim.

Practical Changes

If you tend to think negatively about yourself and criticize yourself often, it is important to begin to eliminate the use of negative labels toward yourself. Cognitively you can tell yourself: *Just because I feel hopeless does not mean that I am hopeless*, or *I feel like a failure, but that does not mean that I am a failure*. We must turn to Scripture to remind us that we are not victims, because God's Word tells us we can have "such confidence as this" because it "is ours through Christ before God" (2 Cor. 3:4). Our confidence comes through Jesus and is ours to keep. Once we have surrendered our lives to Jesus, no matter what our circumstances are, we no longer walk in shame. "Do not be afraid; you will not suffer shame. Do not fear disgrace; you will not be humiliated. You will forget the shame of your youth" (Isa. 54:4). God promises us that He will not shame us if we turn to Him. It is safe to go to God with our shame, because He comforts us.

HOLY PRIESTHOOD

The truth is that we are chosen by God to be loved by Him and to love Him in return. We are being built into a priesthood of people who are pleasing to Him. He says, "As you come to him, the living Stone—rejected by men but chosen by God and precious to him—you also, like living stones, are being built into a spiritual house to be a holy priesthood, offering spiritual sacrifices acceptable to God through Jesus Christ" (1 Pet. 2:4–5).

Isn't that wonderful? We are acceptable to God as we are built together as a holy priesthood. We don't need to go through someone else to connect with God, because we are already connected through Jesus' sacrifice on the cross. If we walk in that confidence, we are walking in the truth that we are *chosen, acceptable, and like living stones* building together a spiritual house (1 Pet. 2:4–5). Even if we are rejected by others, we are chosen by God, precious to God as Jesus is precious to God. Isn't that amazing? I am astounded by that, and comforted to know that I can be confident in that truth whether I feel precious and valued or not. Sometimes we must lean on the truth of God's word when our feelings betray us.

Maybe that was why King David often battled with his emotions and reminded himself of the truth in the Psalms. Sometimes the battle seemed overbearing, and he would cry out, "Why are you downcast, O my soul? Why so disturbed within me? Put your hope in God, for I will yet praise him, my Savior and my God" (Ps. 42:11). We are also reminded in the New Testament that God "comforts the downcast" (2 Cor. 7:6). We can follow King David's example and deliberately place our hope in God's love for us. His acceptance comforts and heals us.

If you are feeling so worn out that you cannot go on, you can find comfort knowing that "A bruised reed he will not break, and a smoldering wick he will not snuff out. In faithfulness he will bring forth justice" (Isa. 42:3). He will bring justice to your situation if you cry out to Him. There have been times in my life when I felt like a smoldering wick barely hanging on to breath and flame. God answered my prayer and carried me through those times, and He brought justice. I have great confidence in my God, my friend and my helper.

HOLD ONTO CONFIDENCE

Once we have this confidence, we are urged to hold onto it. We also have the added incentive that He will reward our confidence. We are told forcibly, "Do not throw away your confidence. It will be richly rewarded. You need to persevere so that when you have done the will of God, you will receive what he has promised" (Heb. 10:35–36). Our confidence will be challenged by life's hardships, by our own cunning mind, by the lies of the enemy, and by the storms we face. Yet God is clear that we must focus on the reward for our perseverance and His promises of eternal love and communion with Him.

We must pull out the weed of a victim mindset, because even if we feel beaten down, or if we face hardship, God is present in our lives to answer our prayers. We must come to His feet and confidently know that He will extend His scepter of grace to us and will gladly embrace us and carry us through. "Dear friends, if our hearts do not condemn us, we have confidence before God and receive from him anything we ask" (1 John 3:21–22). Bring your cares to Him because He cares for you. Trust Him and confess that you struggle with the confidence He gives you by His grace. He will love you in that place, and He will carry you through.

Points to Consider: Victim-hood vs. Confidence

- Experiencing hardships can lead to a victim mindset.
- Pride prevents us from letting go of our victim mindset.
- We can trust God with our feelings, because He will never shame us. Instead He gives us confidence in His love and acceptance.

EXPLORATION QUESTIONS

1. Do I feel like a victim sometimes?
2. What attitudes do I hold onto that contribute to my victim mindset?
3. How can I learn to have my confidence in God's love for me?
4. How can confidence change my attitudes and actions?

FOCUS VERSE

But blessed is the man who trusts in the LORD, whose *confidence* is in him. He will be like a tree planted by the water that sends out its roots by the stream. It does not fear when heat comes; its leaves are always green. It has no worries in a year of drought and never fails to bear fruit.

—Jeremiah 17:7–8, emphasis added

FOCUS PRAYER

Lord, I admit that sometimes I see myself as a victim. I need Your help to change. Help me to put my confidence in Your love for me and to walk in confidence, knowing that Your grace is enough for me. You bore my shame on the cross, and I apologize for continuing to pick it up. Thank you for taking my shame on Yourself. I accept Your sacrifice and need Your help to walk in the confidence that You give me. In Jesus' name, amen.

CHAPTER 5

THE WEED OF
ENTITLEMENT
VS.
THE FRUIT OF
CONTENTMENT

Entitle—To grant somebody the right to have or do something. Or, rights/entitlements to certain kinds of treatment, based on one's status.
—*Encarta Encyclopedia*, 2007

ISN'T IT TRUE that in today's culture we generally feel entitled to special treatment? Whether we are aware of it or not, we all think we deserve special treatment in certain areas of our life. Modern day culture breeds a sense of entitlement through advertising, marketing, and Hollywood culture. We are bombarded with messages that are intended to convince us we deserve special things. With mass media, we see and compare ourselves to others constantly. There are commercials that display images of how things and special treatment can make us happier, and every day when you check out at the grocery store, the magazine racks are filled with images of Hollywood life that give us a distorted view of real life. Even in some social arenas, including churches, there is pressure to compete with others of status for special attention or positions of influence. These things are successful at convincing us that we need to seek wealth and status to be happy.

RIGHTS

Many of us are fortunate enough to have laws that serve to protect our *rights*. It is wonderful to be able to have rights protected. Yet in our entitlement, many of us now want every little right protected. It can get out of hand. For example, I remember going to our favorite pizza place for lunch when I was in high school. We noticed that for the first time we were not given mints at our table. Having garlic breath, we depended on having the mints before we went back to class. So we inquired of the waiter. He let us know that they were being sued by a woman who had cut her tongue on a mint they had given her. We thought, "How ridiculous!" Yet this is often a result of the entitlement culture we live in. When something inconveniences us, many of us are quick to make someone else responsible.

Barraged with messages that prove we have rights to have a bigger home, more accommodating cars, fashionable clothing, comfort, special treatment, and perfect happiness, we become convinced that we need all of these things to be happy. What are your areas of entitlement? Let me give you a hint. It is usually where you find yourself whining the most or what you find yourself longing for. When we feel entitled to something we don't have, we will often whine about it, or sometimes we even become upset that we don't have it, whether it is a thing or the way we are treated.

SPECIAL TREATMENT

My high school boyfriend used to insist on opening the doors for me everywhere I went. If I tried to open the door, he would chastise me and proceed to open the door for me as I walked through. I grew so accustomed to this royal treatment that I began to walk up to doors and pause, waiting for my friends and family to open the door to let me through. It was mostly out of habit, yet my friends would look at me strangely as if to say *why do you think you are so special?* I really wasn't aware that I had unconsciously developed a habit of entitlement waiting for others to open doors for me. Once it was pointed out to me, I realized that what I was doing was, well, a bit supercilious. As a result, I began to make the effort to open the doors for myself.

Similarly, we are often completely unaware of our personal areas of entitlement. We just feel annoyed that others aren't doing what we think they should for us. Possibly someone we trust will point it out to us, or we come into conflict with others and we decide to evaluate our perspective. Many of us hold onto our sense of entitlement for years, somehow feeling that others should know what we need and when we need it and should drop what they are doing to make it happen. That might seem to be a bit of an exaggeration, but often it is not. I have encountered people who live this way, and being around them can be excruciating.

The Challenge of Contentment

Contentment has often been a struggle for me. It is for most of us in some area of our lives. If you are honest with yourself, there is most likely an area of your life in which you struggle with contentment. For me it has been different things at different times in my life. When I was single I sometimes struggled with my desire for a companion. When I lived in an apartment I struggled with the desire for a house. When we have been on a tight budget I have struggled to be content with fewer date nights or not being able to buy new clothes. There are numerous areas in which the struggle for contentment arises. Consider for a moment what your areas of entitlement might be as you become aware of where you are not content.

Is it possible that we are so self-centered we cannot empathize with real people who make real mistakes, or accept real life situations that disappoint us? We don't tolerate when things break down. We cannot accept that finances are tight and we must stick to a budget. Due to our strong sense of entitlement as a culture, we are in an epidemic of credit card debt. The average credit card debt is astounding. We find it challenging to live within our means.

GOD TESTS OUR HEARTS

Sometimes God will test our hearts by temporarily or permanently removing things from our lives that we depend on or feel that we *need*. During those times it is important that we press into God and seek to understand what He is trying to teach us. If we focus only on what we don't have, and what we wish we had, then we will miss the lesson. Growing in contentment brings us closer to God and is an opportunity to look to Him to meet our needs.

The problem with contentment has more to do with our attitudes than anything else. Discontentment breeds frustration since often, when we do attain what we think we must have, we are still left longing for the next thing that we don't have. The Lord is much more interested in the condition of our soul than He is interested in making us comfortable, which is why sometimes He allows us to face the challenge of contentment somewhere in our walk with Him. It does not mean that He is punishing you. Do not give in to the temptation to see it that way. Seek a closer relationship with Him instead, and see where He leads your heart.

Going on a hiking trip up in the Colorado Rocky Mountains with Young Life when I was in high school transformed my view of what I needed. Carrying only two pairs of shorts, two t-shirts, biodegradable soap, enough food for the trip, and sleeping bags, we were stripped to bare minimum. We also had Bibles and carried our tents on our backs. Watches weren't allowed, and obviously, we didn't have cell phones and other gadgets with us. All we had to get where we needed to go were our blistered feet under rugged hiking boots. It was fantastic, and one of the richest times in my life.

Experientially, I grew tremendously on that trip, learning that I needed a lot less than I thought. Without the distractions of things, and the pursuit of things, we grew close as a group and closer to the Lord and His Word. One thing that astounded me was the endless beauty of the mountains, the stars that looked like glitter, and the awesome sunrises. Without distractions we were able to enjoy it all thoroughly. As a group, we bonded and grew in relationship with the Lord. We all commented at the end about how freeing it was not to have so much stuff and that we were surprised at how little you could live on and still thoroughly enjoy life.

That was a volunteer trip that helped me learn the lesson, but there can be other, less pleasant ways life can bring along challenges in contentment. I distinctly remember times in my life that I felt everything I depended on in this life had been shaken up. I had a choice—to press into God or to demand my rights. I have even known people who have become suicidal when they suddenly find themselves on a tight budget. Or I have known of divorces that occur because of financial strain, and a spouse feels entitled to a better life. It's important to seek the Lord when things don't seem to be going your way.

PRIORITY SHIFT

Those times, while difficult, taught me that God really is all that I need and that He is trustworthy. If we choose to cling to our sense of entitlement, we fail to learn the important lessons to be content with what we have on earth, and to shift our priorities to heavenly things. "Do not store up for yourselves treasures on earth, where moth and rust destroy, and where thieves break in and steal. But store up for yourselves treasures in heaven, where moth and rust do not destroy, and where thieves do not break in and steal. For where your treasure is, there your heart will be also" (Matt. 6:19–21). Our hearts must be focused on the fact that this life is temporary and that attaining wealth on earth is short-lived. In our hearts we must be less focused on what we feel we should have now—special treatment, wealth, pampering, nice vacations, convenience—and focus more on what we are looking forward to in heaven—that which is lasting.

JESUS AND HIS GARDENING TOOL

Jesus approaches us with his gardening tool, because He knows we can grow, and He can see what weeds we need to be free from. So often in our shortsightedness we exclaim, "Ouch!" and resist the deep work He is doing in us. We often fail to recognize that although He loves us as we are, He also desires for us to grow and become free from the snares that entangle us. He sees the big picture, while we just see that we are suffering and feel our rights to a convenient life have been imposed on. In those moments it can be greatly productive to ask the Lord, *What are you trying to teach me?* And, *Help me to learn so that I can move forward.* Those moments of surrender of our will allow God to pull the weeds with greater ease and less resistance.

The apostle Paul had probably experienced great wealth before he became a follower of Jesus and a tentmaker. He was a Pharisee and enjoyed high status and most likely all of the conveniences that went along with that. Yet he was able to state:

> I am not saying this because I am in need, for I have learned to be content whatever the circumstances. I know what it is to be in need, and I know what it is to have plenty. I have learned the secret of being content in any and every situation, whether well fed or hungry, whether living in plenty or in want. I can do everything through him who gives me strength.
> —Philippians 4:11–13

Paul not only learned to be content in all circumstances, but also He learned to lean on God for strength. He learned that God is reliable and strong and that all things are possible with God's help and presence in our lives. We like to decorate our homes with phrases like this on plaques. It is good to be reminded that our strength comes from God and not from what we have or can attain. But until we really experience God's strength and truly understand His reliability, meaning doesn't fully bloom or flourish in our hearts.

LEARN THE LESSON

As followers of Jesus we should not be surprised when we are challenged in this area of our life. It is important to root out the entitlement and demands we place on God so we can grow in our faith and trust in Him. I need to inform you that if we don't get the lessons we will continue to experience frustration as we resist what God is trying to teach us. Some of us may even become embittered and feel that because life is unfair, God is unfair.

Our choice to cling to entitlement may result in loss of faith, discouragement, and envy. "A heart at peace gives life to the body, but envy rots the bones" (Prov. 14:30). When we envy others, it affects our inner structure. Our bones enable us to stand. Without a solid bone structure, the other vital functions of the body fall into a heap. If envy "rots the bones," then it certainly must affect all other areas of our spiritual lives. It causes us to lose perspective and shift our priorities away from God and onto other things.

Our strong sense of entitlement may prevent us from knowing God. We mistakenly believe that God should always make sure we are happy or fulfilled, but when we look to earthly things to fill that need, we wonder why He can't satisfy us. We are still in love with things and comforts and status and fail to see that is not what God means when He tells us He will give us the desires of our hearts (see Ps. 37:4). He doesn't mean that you can have that new, red Mustang you would look great in or recognition for your achievements. He means that He will satisfy our souls with a fulfillment that nothing on earth can provide. In our arrogance we think we know what the "desires of our heart" are—it is a new Cuisinart or a big screen TV or a new outfit. We complain in our immature faith when we realize that these are not the "desires of our heart" God is after. He knows you better than you know yourself. He knows that those things will only satisfy you for a moment. He wants to satisfy you deep within your hearts. When our hearts are in alignment with Him, we are then able to ask for things that have lasting value rather than temporary, superficial value.

Spiritual Couch Potatoes

Many of us are actively sitting on our duffs spiritually, not growing in relationship with Him or in understanding of His Word. We are spiritual couch potatoes. Yet when we are in a bind, we cry out to God. It's not that He doesn't hear us; it's that we don't know Him. If we are not in His Word and seeking to know Him better, then we will not understand His will for us. Let's not wait until we are in a bind to reach out to God and then forget about Him again until the next time we are in another bind. None of us like to be treated that way. It feels offensive to us when someone comes to us only when they need something. Yet that is how many of us treat God. Thankfully, He is patient with us. At least we are crying out to Him. We must be willing, though, to allow Him to teach us His way. We must be willing to follow Him. He may lead us down a path we aren't ready to follow, and then we wonder why He hasn't answered our prayer(s). The truth is that He has, but possibly not according to our own formula, so we don't recognize the answer.

God Wants to Bless Us

Blessings and benefits are often things that God gives to those who follow Him wholeheartedly. Luke 12:31 says that if we "seek his kingdom (then) these things will be given (to us) as well." I know of a strong Christian follower who needed a car to get around since he couldn't get to where he needed on his bike any longer. He was on a very tight budget and asked God for a blue car within his price range. A day or so afterward, he happened across a blue car at the

71

exact price he had asked for (an astonishingly low price for a good car). God had blessed him with what he wanted, even down to his favorite color. The Lord "rewards those who earnestly seek Him" (Heb. 11:6). Our priorities must be to seek God and not wealth, accolades, special treatment, or shopping sprees. We trust that as we seek God, what we need and what we want are provided for us along the way.

If we sit on our spiritual duffs and still expect special treatment from God, we are bound to be disappointed. It is important to understand that those who enjoy the perks and blessings of God are those who are in God's will. If we are not actively seeking His presence, His leading, and His direction in our lives, we should not be baffled when our "I need this now" prayers seem not to be heard. He is often silent, waiting for you to come and follow Him.

The truth is that God loves to give gifts to those who love Him and to those who ask Him. I have experienced this first hand many times when specific prayers have been answered. However, when we demand our wishes to be answered, but we are not walking in faith, we get confused. We sort of attend church, we know a thing or two about the Bible, and when we need or want something, we might ask for it in prayer, even though we really aren't interested in following Jesus' call on our life. God impressed on me recently that it is similar to when an employee sits at his desk and does nothing all day but e-mail friends and check his favorite websites. Then he goes to his boss and asks for a raise and a bonus. A wise boss will most likely turn him down—and possibly fire him—for his lack of productivity. The employee feels entitled to special treatment, but won't participate in the basics of the job requirements. If we want to enjoy some of the blessings of God, we need to be actively participating in His work on earth and in prayer about how we can serve others in need.

DEEPER STRUGGLE

There have been times, however, that contentment is a deeper struggle. When we feel entitled to something that we don't have, or to something that has been taken away from us, we become angry and hurt. It becomes easy to lash out at God in anger and frustration. It takes choosing contentment over our human nature and our desires. It means that we struggle daily and confess our lack of gratitude to God in a spirit of repentance until contentment settles in and becomes a reality. Brother Lawrence understood this when he wrote:

> God knows very well what we need and that all He does is for our Good. If we knew how much He loves us, we would always be ready to face life—both its pleasures and its troubles. You know, the difficulties of life do not have to be unbearable. It is the way that we look at them—through faith or unbelief. We must be convinced that our Father is full of love for us and that He only permits trials to come our way for our own good (*The Practice of the Presence of God*).

God is always considering what will benefit us spiritually. We see the short term inconvenience, and God sees what we really need—Him. "For our good" means that He is looking out for what benefits our soul and our eternal inheritance. We look to the material world and fail to see the big picture. God always sees the big picture.

THE BIGGER PICTURE

When my son decided to rock our backyard table until it nearly tipped over and could have landed on his or his sister's head, I put it in the garage. Oh, did he scream when

I did that, but I had told him many times to be responsible with the picnic table. He felt that I was ruining his fun, but I saw a bigger picture than he did, and I was looking out for his safety. God knows when giving us what we want when we want it is going to be harmful to our well-being and our eternal perspective. He is not trying to harm us or ruin our fun. He is protecting the safety of our soul. We must understand that there is much to gain spiritually when we learn contentment:

> But godliness with contentment is great gain. For we brought nothing into the world, and we can take nothing out of it. But if we have food and clothing, we will be content with that. People who want to get rich fall into temptation and a trap and into many foolish and harmful desires that plunge men into ruin and destruction. For the love of money is a root of all kinds of evil. Some people, eager for money, have wandered from the faith and pierced themselves with many griefs.
> —1 Timothy 6:6–10

It is frightening to know that falling in love with money, status, and the conveniences that go along with them can take us away from our life source and eternal hope. No wonder God allows us to be challenged in this area. If we let this weed of discontentment take root in our hearts, it can choke out our faith in Him.

God tells us to focus on His eternal presence in our hearts rather than on earthly things when He says, "Keep your lives free from the love of money and be content with what you have, because God has said, 'Never will I leave you; never will I forsake you.' So we say with confidence, 'The Lord is my helper; I will not be afraid. What can man do to me?'" (Heb. 13:5–6). He is always with us, always loving us and caring for us. He knows what we need, and He always has our best interests at heart. If we are truly seeking God in our lives, He may allow us a season to struggle financially to test our hearts and to challenge us to be content with what we have so that we can focus on what is really important in life—our faith and relationship with Him.

POINTS TO CONSIDER: ENTITLEMENT VS. CONTENTMENT

- In today's culture, many of us feel entitled to special treatment or things.
- Learning contentment deepens our relationship with God and helps us to focus on the hope of heaven.
- God wants to bless us.

EXPLORATION QUESTIONS

1. What do I feel entitled to and why do I feel that way?
2. What drives my entitlement?
3. How can I learn to be content? What do I need to be content about?
4. How will contentment change my life?

FOCUS VERSE

I am not saying this because I am in need, for I have learned to be content whatever the circumstances. I know what it is to be in need, and I know what it is to have plenty. I have learned the secret of being content in any and every situation, whether well fed or hungry, whether living in plenty or in want. I can do everything through him who gives me strength.

—Philippians 4:11–13

Focus Prayer

Lord, I love You, and I am sorry for feeling entitled to special things when I don't deserve them. I am so grateful that You love me and want to give to me what I don't deserve. Help me to be content with what I have and always to be thankful in my heart for what You have given me by Your grace. Thank You for all that You have given to me. I am blessed. In Jesus' name, amen.

CHAPTER 6

THE WEED OF JUDGMENT VS.
THE FRUIT OF COMPASSION

The LORD is good to all; He has compassion on all he
has made.

—Psalm 145:9

UNFORTUNATELY, CHRISTIANS ARE known for their
judgmental attitudes. People shy away from the church
because of the church's tendency to exhibit judgmental
words, actions, and negative facial expressions when we
encounter people in the world. Yet, the Lord we follow is
very firm in His words about judgment and His instructions
for us to refrain from it.

REFRAIN FROM JUDGMENT

Understanding where judgment belongs and where it
does not is of vital importance. If we are quick to judge
others, we undermine the central component of God's
grace and His compassion toward those to whom He longs
to reveal His love. Compassion means to "suffer with" and
indicates primarily that if we are to follow Jesus' example,

we must suffer with others as opposed to being critical of them.

People suffer all kinds of problems, some of them brought on by poor decisions, difficult circumstances, addictive compulsions, or past hurts. Many of us are initially tempted to point out that they should have done things differently, but compassion is much more potent in its ability to bring forth change and growth. Compassion speaks to the heart and does not condemn, but exudes love and care. As believers who are in relationship with God, it is our responsibility to refrain from judging others in our thoughts and actions and to extend grace and mercy instead.

NATURAL TEMPTATION

Why then are we so tempted to pass judgment? It seems to come so automatically that often we are not aware of the toxicity of our attitudes towards others. Have you ever noticed that when you are in a busy mall or crowded place instant conclusions come up as you pass by people, depending on how they dress, how they appear, the color of their skin, style, facial expression, etc.? Without even meeting someone we quickly begin to assess what we think about them based on outer appearance. We are all guilty of this from time to time. When I am stressed or overwhelmed, I fall back into old patterns that I am not always proud of. Thankfully, God's grace meets me when I become aware of it and apologize for passing judgment. He gently convicts and restores.

Just the other day I saw a woman at the grocery store and began to develop a critical attitude toward her. I saw her by her jet black hair, precise haircut, and well-coordinated outfit. She did not seem happy. I was aware that I was creating a judgment of her based on nothing substantial, so

I urged myself to dismiss it. Later, when we ran into each other at the playground, we started a conversation, and I learned some things about her. I learned that she is very sweet and likeable, and my original impression wasn't at all correct. I also learned that she is far away from her family, who live in Europe, which explains why she appeared to be sad.

WHAT GOD SEES

The truth is that we don't know anything about the people we pass by or about their lives. We don't understand what they have been through, how they have been raised, who they really are, or what they can become. God says that He does not look at the outer appearance, but at the heart (see Gal. 2:6). We may think that we know their personality since maybe they have a scowl on their face or their nose up in the air or they appear sad or they are dressed a certain way. We may think judgmental thoughts such as, *What is his problem?* or *She's a stuck up brat* or *What kind of parent's would let their daughter dress that way?* When these moments come, it is important to catch ourselves and shift our thinking. I try to catch myself and think, *That is a person God loves deeply.*

Another time, years ago, when I noticed a very awkward young man worshiping God during a worship service at my church, I began to develop a judgmental attitude toward him. He jerked about and sang too loud and out of tune, and truthfully it made me uncomfortable. As this was happening, I felt the conviction of the Holy Spirit saying that He loves that young man and loves His worship, because his heart is purely worshiping God. Standing corrected by the conviction of the Holy Spirit, I knew then and there that I needed to change my attitude toward the people I

79

encountered around me. Now, before I ever judge, I ask myself what God might think about each person. What would be God's heart for him or her? I deliberately shift my attitude toward recognizing God's love for the people I encounter daily.

We must remember that Jesus hung out with all kinds of "colorful" types. He loved people and reached out to them. His desire is to extend his love and grace to all who come to Him. "Therefore judge nothing before the appointed time; wait till the Lord comes. He will bring to light what is hidden in darkness and will expose the motives of men's hearts. At that time each will receive his praise from God" (1 Cor. 4:5). We are instructed to "wait" and not allow ourselves to judge. God has given all of us many chances to honor Him with our lives, and we must also extend that opportunity to others. It is His job to judge the heart and not the outer appearance, and that is something we are just not able to do because of our human limitations. We must heed the Lord's instruction and step back from our judgmental attitudes.

THE PROBLEM OF PRIDE

When we are prideful, we are often quick to judge. Resistance to God's conviction in our own hearts stems from pride. Arrogantly, we become proud of how well we think we are doing, and as a result, we tend to look down on others. Once we get a handle on our own sinful behaviors and begin to follow God wholeheartedly and do all of the things that Christians should do and stay away from the things Christians shouldn't do, we become proud of ourselves. Smugly, we begin to look down on those who aren't doing everything right. We fail to understand God's grace for those around us who are struggling or still battling addictions, habits, and other issues. I remember in college seeing a friend of mine who was a Christian, and he was smoking. Alarmed, *I thought he was a Christian* went through my mind. I worried about his eternal salvation. This incomprehensible failure to understand God's grace and mercy for him more closely resembled legalism than any true faith in God's unending love.

INSECURITY

On the other hand, we also do this when we feel bad about ourselves. If we are insecure or uncertain about our own abilities, then sometimes we look down on others to feel better about ourselves. This is called *leveling* when we consciously or unconsciously choose to criticize others in order to offset how we really feel about ourselves. We try to bring them down to our level or down to the way we feel about ourselves. When we feel like a failure, we feel comforted when we see that others have failings as well. We point out others, failings in order to feel that we are better than they. This can be very destructive, if done habitually, since you may inadvertently injure your loved ones with unnecessary, critical feedback. This is also rooted in pride and an unwillingness to humbly accept our shortcomings.

If you are a person prone to criticizing others, you may need to explore inwardly what this is about. Does your judgment of others have more to do with your own insecurity than with their shortcomings? If so, seek God's Word on His love for you and find your security in His love and acceptance of you. Even if you aren't living up to your own inner standards, God loves you, and you need to be vulnerable enough to let Him love your wounded and messy parts. When we heal in this area and let God's love invade even our most insecure places, we can extend that same love to others into the wounded places in their hearts and circumstances. Because He loves us deeply even when we have failings, we are able to hope that He can heal us and change us if we let Him.

A CHURCH-WIDE PROBLEM

Unfortunately judgment can be a church-wide problem within congregations. Some churches emphasize following rules apart from God's grace. Many people refer to this as "legalism." In legalistic churches, those who are doing well following the rules will look down on those who are not doing so well. When this becomes a church-wide problem, people are prevented from entering into the community they need because they feel judgment instead of compassion. Due to legalism, congregations can become ingrown and lack the diversity that God's people truly represent, because only those who follow the rules are acceptable.

Judgmental congregations tend to become stale and unsavory. Rather than people "taste(ing) and seeing that the Lord is good" (Ps. 34:8), visitors are made to feel unwelcome and that they don't measure up. I have heard people express that they felt unloved when they visited churches, and therefore, they never returned. In those cases, churches lived up to the stereotypes of what churches are like, and those are the stereotypes that keep people out of churches. Many of the stereotypes are that churches are critical, stingy, dull, rule-bound, and judgmental. People generally don't want to encounter that type of environment. Yet, that is what many people experience when the church fails to recognize and heed what Jesus teaches us about His grace and His compassion. Instead, as we live in God's love and grace, we can joyfully extend God's heart to all people as they enter our churches searching for hope. We have an incredible hope to offer them.

STIFLES OUR WITNESS

Not only does judgment keep people out of our churches where they can grow and be a part of Christian community, but also judging others prevents us from witnessing to them about our faith and hope in Jesus. When we judge others because they are not up to our standards, we fail to see them with God's eyes as someone who needs His grace and love just as much as we do. All we see are the shortcomings. Possibly we notice that they don't dress "properly," or they may suffer an addiction or they may be going through a divorce. Whatever it is, we must toss it aside and choose compassion (see Col. 3:12) instead.

If loving God and one another are our first and second commandments (see Mark 12:31), then the first thing people should encounter when they visit our churches is love rather than judgment. Notably, Scripture emphasizes that even the commandments are intended to be surrounded by love. "The commandments—all of them are summed up in this one rule: 'Love your neighbor as yourself.' Love does no harm to its neighbor. Therefore love is the fulfillment of the law" (Rom. 13:9–10). As a result, we must recognize that loving one another takes precedence over any judgmental attitude, no matter how small.

The truth is that none of us measure up. "All fall short of the glory of God" (Rom. 3:23), and consequently, we all rely on God's grace. Knowing that truth, we need to extend the hand of God's grace to those who visit our churches rather than lining them up on the measuring stick of legalism. When people feel loved, they want to change, when they don't, it is our human nature to rebel. Love has the power to transform, while rules do not.

PLANK IN THE EYE

Jesus is clear that our pride is a plank in our eye that prevents us from seeing others with God's grace and mercy. We see them with judgment instead. He inquires and corrects:

> Why do you look at the speck of sawdust in your brother's eye and pay no attention to the plank in your own eye? How can you say to your brother, "Let me take the speck out of your eye," when all the time there is a plank in your own eye? You hypocrite, first take the plank out of your own eye, and then you will see clearly to remove the speck from your brother's eye.
>
> —Matthew 7:3–5

We need to confess our pride and be humble. If we remove our own pride and arrogance and are humble knowing that "all have sinned and fall short of the glory of God, and are justified freely by his grace through the redemption that came by Christ Jesus" (Rom. 3:23–24), then we are able to truly help each other grow in our faith and walk in truth. The resulting fruit that grows involves being equipped to help others grow in their faith because we understand God's compassion for them. The fruit of compassion is that people experience a bit of God's love and grace, and that witness is more profound and has more impact than anything we try to say to convince them that God is real.

JUDGMENT ROOTED IN SELF-CENTEREDNESS

We also tend to judge from a self-centered perspective rather than from God's perspective. If we don't like to wear high heels, we may judge someone who does, if we don't wear saggy pants, then we may think negatively about someone who does. If we do wear saggy pants with our underwear partially showing, we may judge someone who doesn't dress this way and think they are old-fashioned and obsolete. If we read the Bible everyday, we may judge someone who doesn't. There are as many examples of judgment as there are people. The point is that we mustn't judge from our own eyes, tastes, or preferences. Those are not essential. What matters to God is the heart, and we are not to judge that either.

Every time a judgmental thought enters our minds, we must immediately confess our sin to God and ask for forgiveness. Thankfully, God is patient with us. "But you, O Lord, are a compassionate and gracious God; slow to anger, abounding in love and faithfulness" (Ps. 86:15). Because He is compassionate toward us, we must also be compassionate towards others as an extension of His grace. When we are compassionate towards others, the fruit we bear is the fruit of reaching out to others with the same compassion through which we exist in our daily lives. We can give compassion to others who need it.

PRAYER ANTIDOTE

One way to diminish the impulse to pass judgment on others is to pray for them. I often pray for people I have never met and who I see going about their business. I pray that God will bless them and that they will come to know Jesus more. I pray that God helps them with whatever their struggles are. This helps me to avoid the pull of my rebellious human nature that wants to pass judgment on them. Actively replacing our bad habits with better ones prevents the empty space from getting filled up with either the same bad habit or another one. If we try to force ourselves not to judge, then we will probably continue to do it on a regular basis, because our human nature is so inclined. When you feel the temptation to judge, catch yourself and begin to pray, even if it is only for a moment, for the person you are passing by.

To pull this weed from our lives, we confess our judgments and we pray for those we tend to judge. The result is probably a greater change in us than in the people we pray for, although we may never know how our prayers impact others. We replace our judgments with prayers, and the result is that we begin to have a greater capacity for compassion.

CLOTHING OF COMPASSION

We are commanded not just to keep compassion in our pockets or on the shelf in case we need it or decide to use it. God wants for us to *wear* it. "Therefore, as God's chosen people, holy and dearly loved, *clothe* yourselves with compassion" (Col. 3:12, emphasis mine). We make compassion about who we are. Just like our style of clothing says something about our personalities, compassion, when we wear it daily, says something about our identity with Jesus and the fact that we are "dearly loved." God extends His love towards others through our compassion for the people He loves, which includes the awkward man with the mismatched outfit, the woman in the wheelchair, the teenager with the black leather boots and long black jacket, the girl with the too short skirt, and the refugee from a war-ridden country.

When we wear compassion as a character trait, it comes easily to extend God's love and forgiveness to others. The love of the Lord radiates out of us, and others notice. They see the hope that we have in our hearts and are drawn toward the Lord because they see something different in us. People can generally tell if we are sincere or not. If we are not in a stance of readiness to extend compassion to others the Lord brings across our path, they may miss finding the hope the Lord longs to extend to non-believers through us.

ISOLATION FROM COMMUNITY

A primary consequence of judgment is isolation. It prevents people from experiencing community, and community offers support, nurturing, prayer, practical help, understanding, comfort, and many other blessings. When we judge others, we prevent them from feeling comfortable in community, and the result is isolation. When people are isolated they are more prone to depression, anxiety, spiritual attack, suicide, loneliness, hopelessness, divorce, and other negative costs of isolation.

When I encourage clients to get more involved in community, I have heard many of them say they don't get involved in community because they feel judged. I feel helpless in these situations, because I know how life-giving community can be, yet when people feel judgment instead of compassion, seclusion is the result. The enemy wants us to be isolated because then we are more prone to losing hope when we struggle. Others help us to retain hope when we don't have it for ourselves. In community we hear, "You are going to get through this," "I care about you," "Can I pray for you?" or "Can I bring you a meal?" These are small things that add up and help us grow in our faith and endurance when hardship comes.

WE NEED EACH OTHER

Refrain from judging so that others can be a part of the community and its rich resources that they need in ways they cannot describe and ways you are not aware of. We need to be cognizant of how much we need each other. "And let us consider how we may spur one another on toward love and good deeds. Let us not give up meeting together, as some are in the habit of doing, but let us encourage one another, and all the more as you see the Day approaching" (Heb. 10:24–25). We all need community to encourage and help each other, because we all face hardships.

Others of us may create isolation for ourselves because we judge those who might be a support for us and a part of the community with which God surrounds us. Sometimes God brings people into our lives so that we can grow and because they will challenge us out of our comfort zones. We must be willing to give them a chance to be in our lives and not just seek out people who are like us. If we surround ourselves with people who are the same socio-economically, ethnically, spiritually, and otherwise the same, we miss out on the richness of God's diverse design and opportunities to share our faith.

When we judge others, we are cooperating with the enemy and His plans to divide and prevent people from coming into relationship with God. It is extremely prideful to judge others and costly to yourself and to others.

FOR OUR OWN BENEFIT

There is a selfish motive in refraining from judging others as well. Scripture is clear that "in the same way you judge others, you will be judged" (Matt. 7:1). If we do not want to be judged by God on our own judgment day, then we must not judge others. The primary reason we judge others is pride, because "if we claim to be without sin, we deceive ourselves and the truth is not in us" (1 John 1:8). It is important to remain humble and always to recognize that none of us is without sin. We all have fallen short of what God's law requires, yet God loves to give us His grace. Because we receive His grace, we must not forsake it by judging others. Judging others is the primary blockade to receiving God's grace and mercy that we all need. It is a choice that we have—judge and be judged, or give grace and receive grace. It's a very simple formula, but one that we seem to struggle with constantly. We must keep in mind that God plans to bless us if we follow this instruction:

> Finally, all of you, live in harmony with one another; be sympathetic, love as brothers, be compassionate and humble. Do not repay evil with evil or insult with insult, but with blessing, because to this you were called so that you may inherit a blessing.
> —1 Peter 3:8–9

He reminds us to remember that He wants to bless us with an inheritance in heaven, and that motivates us to pull out this weed and not to be complacent about it. If we are lazy in our efforts to root out the weed of judgment and fail to be compassionate, we miss out on a blessing that we cannot yet see but for which we hope.

NOT OUR PLACE

When Jesus was teaching at the Mount of Olives, the Pharisees attempted to trap Jesus by bringing Him a woman they caught in the act of adultery:

> They made her stand before the group and said to Jesus, "Teacher, this woman was caught in the act of adultery. In the Law Moses commanded us to stone such women. Now what do you say?" Jesus bent down and started to write on the ground with his finger. When they kept on

questioning him, he straightened up and said to them, "If any one of you is without sin, let him be the first to throw a stone at her." Again he stooped down and wrote on the ground. At this, those who heard began to go away one at a time, the older ones first, until only Jesus was left, with the woman still standing there. Jesus straightened up and asked her, "Woman, where are they? Has no one condemned you?" "No one, sir," she said. "Then neither do I condemn you," Jesus declared. "Go now and leave your life of sin."

—John 8:4–11

Understanding that it is not our place to judge others is critical. None of us can stand before God and say that we haven't sinned. That truth should cause us to remain humble. Even if we aren't outwardly judgmental, God knows our inner thoughts, and we must confess to Him our critical attitude.

We must recognize that only Jesus has the capacity to judge because the Father has given Him the authority: "He has given him authority to judge because He is the Son of Man" (John 5:27). We see in the story above that He wants to extend his grace first and foremost because He "did not come to judge the world, but to save it" (John 12:47). Jesus' first priority always is to minister to the people around Him and not to place judgment on them. He gives everyone a chance to change.

MERCY TRIUMPHS

Jesus became very angry when religious leaders placed judgment on people rather than compassion. When we judge others, we develop a Pharisee's heart. A heart that is hardened and willful and full of pride. We must understand that God's character is "full of compassion and mercy"

(James 5:11). Scripture is clear that we should "speak and act as those who are going to be *judged by the law that gives freedom,* because judgment without mercy will be shown to anyone who has *not* been merciful. Mercy triumphs over judgment!" (James 2:12–13, emphasis mine). We need to be mindful of that fact and give mercy to others freely and without inhibition.

Triumph also means victory. Isn't that a powerful statement—that "mercy triumphs over judgment?" When we are merciful, we position ourselves to receive mercy. I don't know about you, but I know for a fact that I am desperately in need of mercy! Mercy and compassion must be a priority for us, because it overrides judgment. It is the ace of spades!

The enemy wants us to pass judgment on each other because we not only forfeit our own ability to receive mercy, but also we fail to extend mercy to others who need it. It is a double loss, a loss for ourselves and a loss for those whom God desires us to reach with compassion and grace. On the other hand, it is a bountiful harvest for us if we are able to pull out this weed, because not only do we get to experience God's love and compassion, but also others in our lives do as well. People's lives are changed when they encounter compassion. Knowing this should encourage us to gladly live lives of compassion for others.

JESUS OUR EXAMPLE

Jesus is our ultimate example for how to use compassion in our lives. Everywhere Jesus went, Scripture says He had compassion for the people. It is from the posture of compassion that He ministered and healed those who came to Him. People also felt at ease coming to Him in large crowds because He was compassionate. It made Him approachable and safe to be with. He wanted to guide them and provide shelter for them: "When he saw the crowds, he had compassion on them, because they were harassed and helpless, like sheep without a shepherd" (Matt. 9:36). It was the Lord's heart to provide shelter from the harassment of life's troubles.

When we respond to His compassion for us, we are provided with shelter and healing. Whenever Jesus healed people, His healing was extended through the sentiment of compassion. "He had compassion on them and healed their sick" (Matt. 14:14). Compassion is a deep love and concern for others. And it is a trait we should be seeking to replicate in our interactions with others. It is a completely opposing concept from judgment. Judgment separates, while compassion draws and brings us together.

We are all a part of the community of believers, and those who are not yet believers are still people on whom Jesus has compassion. Jesus said to them, "'It is not the healthy who need a doctor, but the sick. I have not come to call the righteous, but sinners'" (Mark 2:17). Jesus loved to hang out with broken, hurting, confused people who needed Him, and He came under great criticism for it. Why then should we as followers of Jesus love and hang out only with each other?

In contrast, we should be interacting with many different people out of a heart of compassion, with the hope that they will see their need for God's love in their lives. Compassion has an impact in and of itself. We might think, *I can't lay my hands on a blind man and make him see,* so we give up our efforts to minister to others. (Hmm…a little perfectionism creeping in.) Yet we are called to become more like Jesus as we follow Him, and that means that we need to clothe ourselves with compassion and heal the sick. All God requires is a little willingness. He is able to do the rest.

SOW COMPASSION

I once prayed for a lady with chronic back problems, and as I was praying, she said she felt tremendous heat on her back and said her back felt better. I never had a chance to follow up with her, but I know that the Holy Spirit was at work. I did my part by having compassion and praying for her, and the Holy Spirit came in and did His part. I have heard many current stories of people being healed physically when people chose to pray.

Possibly the healing someone needs is not physical, but emotional or psychological or practical. What we need to be doing as believers is to have compassion on whomever God brings across our path that needs His love. That doesn't mean you become overly invested in their lives, you must have healthy boundaries. It means that you listen, you genuinely care, and you pray. If you are able to help practically, do it by giving food, clothing, and help. Do not judge them for their circumstances, how they dress, how much they drink, or their weight, but care about them as Jesus does, and you may witness a miracle...a transformation.

Your kindness towards them might not do anything until years later. They might remember and consider and give God a chance because you showed them a sample of God's love. If you have experienced God's love and grace in your life, all it takes is sharing a little of that with others instead of being quick to criticize. Do not "size up" the people around you. Rather, show them compassion because Jesus has shown you compassion. If you do this, you will bear fruit from the compassion that you share with others.

POINTS TO CONSIDER: JUDGMENT VS. COMPASSION

- Judging others is a natural temptation.

- Judging others prevents them from experiencing God's grace and compassion.
- When we are compassionate, God brings healing to their hearts.

EXPLORATION QUESTIONS

1. Am I judgmental? In what areas am I judgmental?
2. What drives my judgmental attitudes?
3. How can I change my judgmental attitudes into compassion?
4. How has Jesus had compassion on me?
5. How can I benefit from compassion?

FOCUS VERSE

For this very reason, Christ died and returned to life so that he might be the Lord of both the dead and the living. You, then, why do you judge your brother? Or why do you look down on your brother? For we will all stand before God's judgment seat. It is written: "As surely as I live," says the Lord, "every knee will bow before me; every tongue will confess to God."

—Romans 14:9–11

FOCUS PRAYER

Lord, forgive me for having an attitude of judgment toward others. I am sorry that I look down on others. Help me to see others with the love that You have for them. Thank You for having compassion on me. Help me to also extend Your compassion towards others. In Jesus' name, amen.

CHAPTER 7

THE WEED OF ANGER
VS.
THE FRUIT OF
FORGIVENESS

ANGER, A POTENT emotion, can lead us into destructive places in our souls. Most of us have been acquainted with anger of varying degrees during our lives. I can tell you that I have been thoroughly challenged in this area of my life. If you have ever felt angry before and struggled to truly forgive, this chapter is important.

What we get angry about says a lot about what is important to us. Some things are truly worth getting angry about, while other things are not. Our anger may honestly reflect how we feel. We may feel that we have been wronged or someone we care about has been wronged. Often anger is a reaction to injustice or hurt, or to feeling misunderstood, unloved, and betrayed.

In other cases, our ego may be bruised and we feel angry because our weakness is exposed. We are not ready to admit our weaknesses, so instead we lash out and accuse others. Often anger has more to do with feelings of hurt than it does about anything else. Our first reaction is anger, but if we stop and think about how we are really feeling, often it is hurt, disappointment, betrayal, or any other primary emotion that fuels the anger.

BURIED ANGER

Sometimes when we are angry, we bury our anger deep down in the caverns of our soul and convince ourselves it doesn't affect us. It is important to understand that nothing could be further from the truth. If you bury your feelings and smile politely to the people in your life, your anger is guaranteed to re-surface toward another person, object, or situation that has nothing to do with your original source of anger.

Many of us who have grown up in dysfunctional homes (because of sin all families have some type of dysfunction to varying degrees) have learned to bury our hurts deep down inside of us while we put on a mask in front of others to show that we are doing great. I have heard this dynamic called the "smiling depressed." Our pain only deepens when we force ourselves to suppress it, although we may appear to be happy on the outside. I lived this way for many years. Often feeling a great deal of pain on the inside, I would smile politely to everyone around me. When we do this, we alienate ourselves from others who can support us and help us. Inside we ache and long for healing, but we often don't understand where it comes from because we haven't dealt with it.

DISPLACED ANGER

Buried anger shows up at random times that are often unrelated to what the anger is truly about. Have you ever flown off the handle about something only to wonder where all of that rage came from? Or maybe you were on the receiving end of rage and wondering, *What in the world was that?* You know that the anger expressed was way out of proportion to the actual situation. What happens when we stuff our anger is that it begins to accumulate and begins to shift from appropriate anger to buried rage from years of un-dealt-with hurts. It will then surface un-expectedly and often inappropriately onto unrelated people, situations, or things. In psychology this has been called the "kick–the-dog syndrome" because someone may "kick the dog" when, for example, he or she is mad at a friend for not coming to a party.

Depending on how deeply the hurts get buried, there may be little or no insight into the fact that "kicking the dog" had anything to do with feeling hurt. Some of us are better at burying our anger than others.

When we take out our anger on others who are unrelated to what we are angry about, the emotion is also known as *displaced anger*. Sometimes when we are unable to deal directly with our anger because we feel threatened by someone we are angry with, it gets taken out on others who are less threatening. When we really are mad at a situation or person, and we feel out of control and unable to resolve the problem, we may turn on an assistant and chew out that person for not making enough copies. The assistant is confused. You, meanwhile, may feel some relief, even though the true situation has not been dealt with. When we feel unable to directly handle our pain, it is easier to let it off on someone or something less threatening to us.

Passive Aggression

Someone who has buried rage may appear meek and happy on the outside. However, this can be covering for anger, and those close to this individual will notice passive-aggressive behavior or inappropriate anger outbursts. *Passive aggression* appears when an individual is not able to appropriately discharge or resolve feelings of anger, and they begin to act in ways that loved ones find exasperating, such as chronic lateness, burning food, or sabotage.

Now keep in mind that burned food or lateness does not always indicate buried anger or resentment, so please do not jump to conclusions when this happens from time to time. However, there are times when this truly is the outlet for buried anger. Some of us do it habitually, much to the frustration of those around us, and many of us, if we are honest, have occasionally let ourselves be passive-aggressive when we were angry with someone. Passive aggression can be as mild as burning the toast, or as severe as having an affair. What it really indicates is that there is unresolved anger.

Other factors may contribute to such things. I do specifically remember a time when I was dating someone and became angry due to a pattern of lateness, miscommunication, and blame. I realized while preparing a steak dinner that was about to be overcooked, that I didn't care. I seemed inwardly pleased, since I was pretty sure he would criticize my cooking anyway—which he did. This is an example of passive-aggression in action. Many of us do this from time to time when we are upset. However, some of us do this so often, and have so successfully buried years of anger, that we are not even able to connect our behavior with our feelings. We are not even aware that what we are doing is linked to our emotions. Nor are we aware of how destructive it can be to our relationships.

WHY THIS IS IMPORTANT

I share all of this because it is important to understand what results when anger is not addressed appropriately. We deceive ourselves when we think that if we just ignore it or "sweep it under the rug" it will go away. Why then do we tend to avoid dealing with our anger appropriately? It would seem that we would be eager to resolve anger if it is so important to keep our relationships intact and to ensure that we are benefiting from the blessings of healthy and honest relationships. Yet, we are all prone to avoid direct communication for a variety of reasons. Some of us avoid it because it is uncomfortable for us. Anger is a strong emotion, and we fear losing control or losing relationship. We may fear that our true feelings will be rejected or laughed at, which would add to our hurt, so we keep it to ourselves.

POOR ROLE MODELS

Another reason we avoid anger is due to poor role modeling. Many of us learned in childhood that it is not okay to express anger because our parents modeled emotional suppression or because we were taught it is wrong to let our anger out. We may have been made fun of or told our feelings were stupid, so we learned that it is safer to hide our emotions then to express them. Some of us have been exposed to erratic expressions of anger and abusive outbursts of rage that leave us stunned and uncertain. As a result of our experience with poor examples of dealing with anger, we don't trust ourselves with the emotion. Stuffing it seems easier.

Again, anger is usually a secondary emotion. It signals that something else has happened. Possibly you were hurt by what someone said to you, or you may have felt invalidated or misunderstood. Sometimes things outside our control happen and we direct our anger toward the people involved, such as in a car accident. Other times we feel betrayed by the people we love and lose our equilibrium. There are degrees of hurt from minor infractions to pre-meditated actions that anger us. Typically, anger hits close to the heart when it involves people you care about. There can be many reasons why we feel anger.

OVER-EXPRESSION OF ANGER

Others of us don't have much of a problem expressing our anger. We wear our "hearts on our sleeves," and when we feel angry, everyone around us knows about it. We might lash out at the one whom we are angry with by yelling. Or we may openly criticize the person with whom we are angry with. We may choose more subtle forms of expression such as sending glares and hostility toward them.

Abuse often occurs when people have difficulty control-ling their anger. People can call others horrible names. They can hit, shove, kick, and throw. This is very traumatizing for those who experience it and those who witness it. Children who witness the abuse of their parents towards each other will exhibit many of the same trauma symptoms as a child who has been directly abused. When anger reaches this level, drastic measures need to be taken to protect those involved, especially children.

If you are aware of this kind of abuse, you can make an anonymous call to the Department of Child and Family Services to ensure that children are safe. Many fear that it automatically means the children will be taken out of the home and placed in foster care, but often that is not the case. Counseling and instruction are often mandated for parents, and an assessment is made about the safety in the home. Generally the services try to keep children with the parents unless the abuse is severe enough to warrant the children being removed from the home. Even then, they give parents time to demonstrate they are able to control their anger and care for their children. Please do not stand idly by if you are aware of physical abuse in a home.

APPROPRIATE USE OF ANGER

Anger in itself is not a wrong emotion to have, but what we do with our anger is very important. Jesus commands us to "not sin in your anger" (Eph. 4:26). This is a warning to refrain from allowing anger to control our actions in destructive and impulsive ways. How we conduct ourselves during our heightened emotion of anger is critical. This does not mean we suppress our anger…we must look to God for direction and wisdom for how to appropriately work through it and forgive those who have hurt us.

Remember that if we suppress rather than forgive, we put ourselves at risk for storing up unresolved anger, which will inevitably result in future anguish. Please understand that there is a very significant difference between truly forgiving others in our hearts and suppressing our emotions until they simmer into a rage so that we aren't even in touch with ourselves. That anger will be released at another time or will be expressed through passive-aggressive actions or displaced anger that will be confusing to you and to your loved ones. Our inner turmoil will negatively affect our relationships whether we admit it or not.

There really are three important things we can do to handle our feelings appropriately. First, we must acknowledge that the anger exists within us and be honest with ourselves regarding what it is about. If we are angry at a friend, a co-worker, a parent, a child, a spouse, or a situation outside of our control, we need to be truthful about what has upset us. It is impossible to forgive, unless you first acknowledge what has hurt you. Ask yourself some questions to identify the source of your anger. Questions such as: What am I angry about? Why did I react that way? What does that mean? What can I do about it?

Second, if you have a chance, you need to approach the person with whom you are angry and let him or her know you are hurt by something he or she did or said. It is a good idea to think ahead about what you might say to that person. Then speak with the intention of moving toward resolution rather than taking revenge or merely letting off steam. This can be done by phone, with a letter, or in person. If the situation seems volatile and you think you or the other party may become easily provoked—if it doesn't feel safe to speak with the person—then I recommend writing a letter. Once you have written the letter, walk away from it and have someone else that you trust proofread it for you. Then go back and make changes so you are able to communicate effectively without attacking the other person. Let the person know how you feel and why and how you wish things were different.

Thirdly, you need to forgive them and let it go. Forgiveness can be very challenging depending on the situation and the type of wound you have experienced. Also, it can be challenging if the abuse is ongoing and your efforts to resolve it are met with further injury. If you are having trouble forgiving, you may need to ask others to pray for you, memorize scripture about forgiveness, and pray for God's help. Forgiveness can be challenging, although it is something that should be pursued wholeheartedly.

WHAT FORGIVENESS IS NOT

Many of us are unable to forgive because we don't really understand what forgiveness is. Forgiveness is not being a "doormat" or letting someone "off the hook" for what they did to you. It is not resignation that will allow it to happen again. Forgiveness does not mean you are saying that what was done to you was okay. Instead, forgiveness actually acknowledges that a wrong was done. It formalizes and makes it clear that you were injured, sinned against, betrayed, lied to, mistreated, or in other ways caused pain. However, in spite of your deep inner hurt, you are choosing forgiveness over revenge, resentment, or hostility. Truly the lack of forgiveness in our hearts is severely caustic to our well-being in a variety of ways—physically, emotionally, relationally, and even psychologically.

Forgiveness is not easy. It can be one of the biggest challenges we face. I am the type of person who endures a lot and generally doesn't let small things get to me. But there are certain areas that challenge me much more deeply when it comes to forgiveness. If someone were to steal my jacket, I would be bothered by it, but I have learned to let that go, because it's only a jacket after all. Jackets can be replaced, or we can live without them. Yet, if it involves something more close to the heart, it becomes much more deeply challenging. For example, there was a family who was hit by a reckless, drunken driver as they walked across the street here in Denver. The husband was the only survivor and faced the tragic and sudden loss of his wife and two children after his recovery in the hospital. As a believer, he stated publicly that he was able to forgive the men who were responsible. Forgiving a pain of that magnitude is only something that can be done with the help and love of the Holy Spirit. The pain he experiences daily has to be tremendous, but the hope of heaven and God's grace gave him the strength to do the impossible.

I know that for victims of molestation, forgiveness can be a lifelong struggle and the pain resilient. It involves not only forgiving the molester, but also often others who may have known but didn't protect you. Fortunately, I have not experienced that pain, although I know that for those who have the pain is tremendous.

PRESS INTO FORGIVENESS

Personally, I have had trouble forgiving when the event involves my loved ones—my husband or children. I think that this is true for a lot of us. When the people we love more than anything are hurt because of something or someone, anger wells up inside of us that is powerful and can be overwhelming. It can also be very difficult to let go of. It can be particularly difficult if the result was a death or significant loss. Some of us have experienced the death of a loved one, and the pain is devastating. Forgiving those involved in that death can be hard because of the depth of the pain. Yet, Scripture is very clear about forgiveness. We need to press into it, even when we really don't want to. There is nothing too severe to be forgiven, and once we have forgiven, a greater depth of healing takes place, and we are often then able to minister to others in similar circumstances.

THE COST OF NOT FORGIVING

Forgiveness is important for many reasons. And understanding what un-forgiveness does to us is an important concept to grasp as well, so that in the situations some of us have to face, we can forgive. Un-forgiveness tears at the heart and soul not of the one who needs to be forgiven, but the one who won't forgive. I know because I have experienced not only the emotional consequences of un-forgiveness, but also physical symptoms as well. Un-forgiveness can cause us to hate, to harbor resentment, to become bitter, and to develop physical and psychological symptoms as well. We can have difficulty sleeping, develop ulcers, experience depression, become anxious, and become pre-occupied with our hurt. It can rob us of the joy that our life in relationship with Jesus was intended to be. It is impossible to experience joy when we are bogged down by un-forgiveness. Forgiving will allow you to experience the joy of God's presence.

SO WE CAN BE FORGIVEN

It is also important to forgive others so that we can be forgiven by God. God is very clear that He wants us to forgive others so that He can forgive us. If we choose not to forgive others, we will forfeit our opportunity to receive the forgiveness that we all so desperately need. "For if you forgive men when they sin against you, your heavenly Father will also forgive you. But if you do not forgive men their sins, your Father will not forgive your sins" (Matt. 6:14–15). This verse has been critical for me at times when I was hurting so much and was so angry that I didn't want to forgive and felt I couldn't forgive. I knew deep down that I could forgive and that I needed to forgive, but I had to press into the Holy Spirit and God's Word to get me there.

Are you hurting? Are you angry at someone or something? Are you having trouble forgiving? Sometimes it isn't easy, but it is important. It often doesn't happen in a moment. It can be a process by which we continue to choose forgiveness day after day until it really takes hold in our heart. Forgiveness replaces bitterness. Forgiveness allows us to live again. Forgiveness heals our hearts.

I remember a time period when I struggled with un-forgiveness for more than a year. I continued to work deliberately toward forgiveness, knowing it needed to be done. I cried out to God to help me forgive, because I knew that in my own power I just couldn't do it. I knew He was helping me, but in the midst of my hurting heart, I still had trouble. I read verses about forgiveness. I prayed. I asked my friends to pray. I asked my church to pray. I pursued forgiveness even when it evaded me. I remember the moment when my heart shifted. It had been a long process and months of deliberately trying to forgive, when finally I felt a tangible shift in my spirit. I rejoiced and thanked God because I knew in that moment the forgiveness I had found was real. I had finally and truly gotten there. I called the person I needed to forgive to demonstrate to myself that it had truly occurred. Interestingly, that person had just walked in the door, and we were able to talk briefly.

KEEP SETTING IT DOWN

I wish I could say that I never picked up un-forgiveness again, but there were still moments that I would relive what had happened, and anger and hurt would bubble back up to the surface as I ruminated over it. However, since I had gotten to a new place in my heart, I was quick to catch myself and refused to mull it over in my mind and spirit. I could feel it's toxicity in me, and I made myself choose forgiveness again and again. As I practiced letting it go, I felt great relief and renewal in my spirit. Since then a lot of restoration has occurred between us, for which I am grateful.

FREEDOM IN FORGIVENESS

True forgiveness sets you free from your burden and turns it over to God. It also builds character in us and binds us together. We are instructed to "bear with each other and forgive whatever grievances you may have against one another. Forgive as the Lord forgave you. And over all these virtues put on love, which binds them all together in perfect unity" (Col. 3:13–14). We forgive because we have been forgiven. I forgave because I wanted to continue to be forgiven, because I know that I am a sinner.

I know that I need God's grace. We all need God's grace, and we are all capable of hurting one another. None of us deserved forgiveness from God, but He forgives because He loves us. We forgive others not because they deserve it, but because we have been forgiven even though we don't deserve God's love and forgiveness.

WHAT IF THEY NEVER APOLOGIZE?

When I have struggled with un-forgiveness, I have wondered, do I forgive only when they ask me to forgive them and admit to what they did. *Is it okay to stay angry if they never ask for forgiveness?* I looked at the verse. "If your brother sins, rebuke him, and if he repents, forgive him. If he sins against you seven times in a day, and seven times comes back to you and says, 'I repent,' forgive him." (Luke 17:3–4). I thought, "Okay, if there is repentance then forgive." But I wondered what if he or she doesn't repent? Do I have to forgive then?

The lack of repentance can make the struggle to forgive even more challenging. It not only hurts when something bad happens to us and our feelings are hurt, but also when whomever is involved doesn't apologize or even turns the blame onto us, it continues to hurt so deeply that we are tempted to lash out or to refuse to forgive. We convince ourselves that they don't deserve forgiveness, and we justify our unforgiving heart.

However, Scripture warns against harboring ongoing anger. "Refrain from anger and turn from wrath; do not fret—it leads only to evil" (Ps. 37:8). We are urged to keep our impulses in check. "A fool gives full vent to his anger, but a wise man keeps himself under control" (Prov. 29:11). If we do not refrain from letting anger deepen in our hearts, it may lead to destructive choices, additional hurtful actions, and ongoing inner hurt. In extreme cases it can lead to injury or to murder. Therefore we need to pursue forgiveness in all cases, whether or not there has been repentance. However, if a genuine apology has not been made firm, boundaries need to be put into place and council is needed regarding how to proceed.

ROOM FOR GOD'S WRATH

In addition, we need to allow room for God to work and not take His work into our own hands. Only God knows the motives of hearts, and only God can make a judgment about what is appropriate for that person:

> Do not repay anyone evil for evil. Be careful to do what is right in the eyes of everybody. If it is possible, as far as it depends on you, live at peace with everyone. Do not take revenge, my friends, but leave room for God's wrath, for it is written: "It is mine to avenge; I will repay," says the Lord. On the contrary: "If your enemy is hungry, feed him; if he is thirsty, give him something to drink. In doing this, you will heap burning coals on his head." Do not be overcome by evil, but overcome evil with good.
> —Romans 12:17–21

On the contrary, we are commanded to do what we can only do with God's help—be kind to our enemies. We are not to take revenge or lash out at or seek to pay back. We must trust that only God knows the motive of their hearts, and only God can truly address the situation appropriately. When we choose to do what we do not want to do and can only do with God's strength, then we not only give room for God's wrath, but also we demonstrate God's love for others through our actions. It gives them an opportunity to feel convicted and to repent. I believe that I have seen God's intervention take place when the choice has been made not to take revenge. Even if you don't witness God's intervention, you need to trust that God can and will take care of it appropriately.

It is not up to you to make them repent. However, we need to have healthy boundaries. Confrontation might be necessary, and we are exhorted to admonish. Their response is up to them. God will deal with them accordingly. It is also important in some relationships to set up boundaries that need to be maintained to provide safety for all involved.

BOUNDARIES

If there has been sexual misconduct or molestation, it is even more essential to establish and maintain boundaries. You cannot, under any circumstances, risk re-injury or someone else being injured. You can forgive the offender, but you must not give them an opportunity to harm you or anyone else again. Setting up boundaries does not mean that you are not forgiving them. It means you are being smart and protecting yourself or your loved ones from harm. Abuse is life-altering and emotionally damaging. Without an apology, you have no reassurance that change has occurred in the abuser, and you need to respond accordingly with boundaries and clearly stated expectations. If boundaries are not respected, then you need to have a plan B in place and be ready to follow through on it since your children need you to protect them.

GET RID OF ANGER

> And do not grieve the Holy Spirit of God with whom
> you were sealed for the day of redemption. Get rid of
> all bitterness, rage and anger, brawling and slander along
> with every form of malice. Be kind and compassionate
> to one another, forgiving each other, just as in Christ
> God forgave you.
>
> —Ephesians 4:30–32

The Bible is clear that when we are bitter, angry, and hostile toward others, it grieves the Holy Spirit. We are commanded not just to avoid "rage and anger, brawling and slander, along with every form of malice" but to "get rid of" it (Eph. 4:30–31). To *get rid of it* implies deliberate action on our part to discard it and take it out to the trash. We are not to be tolerant of it in our minds and spirits. If it is there, we need to deal with it. "Sweeping it under the rug" is not dealing with it. It is avoiding it. We must admit that we are angry, bring it to God, and choose to forgive. We must refuse to payback evil for evil, rather, we must extend kindness to our enemies.

It is impossible to know how challenging this is until you have been face to face with it. Some of you know firsthand this challenge. Just because it is difficult, does not mean we can avoid it. We must deal harshly with our own pain and un-forgiveness by experiencing first God's grace for us, and then by extending that grace to others. We can only do this through the love and help of the Holy Spirit. With His help we are able to demonstrate how abundant and wonderful God's grace truly is.

We must not "let any unwholesome talk come out of (our) mouths, but only what is helpful for building others up according to their needs, that it may benefit those who listen" and we must "be kind and compassionate to one another, forgiving each other, just as in Christ God forgave you" (Eph. 4:29, 32).

THE PORTRAIT OF AN APOLOGY

Not only must we learn to forgive others, but also we must learn to apologize when we have wronged someone. We often become so concerned with the fact that we have not been approached with an apology that we fail to recognize our own flawed attitudes, insensitive comments, hurtful actions, and our own failures. We are not perfect, and therefore, we all have times when we need to apologize to others.

There is usually a strong temptation to hope no one noticed what we said or did, even if we feel convicted. We let time go by and hope others will forget. I know because I have faced this temptation. I have said or done things I have regretted, and sometimes I have been too uncomfortable to apologize, so I let it pass. Other times I have chosen to speak up and apologize and have found that my anxiety about apologizing almost always was out of proportion with the kind response I got in return. Sometimes I hear, "I didn't even notice." Other times there is a genuine relief and restoration of relationship.

This is different from what is called the "I'm sorry" syndrome. The "I'm sorry" syndrome is when someone apologizes all of the time for everything, even things that don't apply to you. I used to do this when I was younger. I felt so bad about myself that I tended to automatically apologize for everything. My friends would become annoyed with me and say, "Stop saying you're sorry," and of course I would reply with an "I'm sorry." They would laugh at my apology for being sorry.

Being self-aware and able to genuinely apologize when you have wronged someone is critical for maintaining close and happy relationships. Even if someone has chosen to forgive without an apology, the lack of an apology will put a wedge of mistrust in a relationship. If you wonder why your adult kids don't open up to you or why your marriage is in trouble or why your friend doesn't call you anymore, maybe an apology is a good place to start. If you have a general idea of what to apologize for, then do it. It can be messy and a bit awkward. You might be profoundly surprised by how a good apology can bring back trust and resolution to years of pain and hurt. If you have no idea, then ask and give the person an opportunity to explain what you might need to apologize for. If he or she doesn't tell you, then you can apologize for "whatever it is you did to hurt him or her," or let the person know that when he or she is ready to tell you, you would love to hear what it is.

(If there is anyone out there that I have hurt through my words or my actions or both, please let me know. I would love to have an opportunity to apologize to you personally.

I can think of some people I would like to have that chance with, but don't have your contact information. I am sorry for anything that I might have said or done that was hurtful. Throughout my life I have been in various stages of my journey out of the weeds, and I have not always acted in ways that are healthy in the past. I still revert back to old patterns when I am tired or weary. I am sorry for that.)

BEAR WITH ONE ANOTHER

Out of a place of humility we realize that we need God's grace, and we also need to extend grace to people around us. The apostle Paul instructs us, "Therefore, as God's chosen people, holy and dearly loved, clothe yourselves with compassion, kindness, humility, gentleness and patience. Bear with each other and forgive whatever grievances you may have against one another. Forgive as the Lord forgave you. And over all these virtues put on love, which binds them all together in perfect unity" (Col. 3:12–14). This verse has ministered to me during times when I was having a hard time forgiving. I wrote it on a piece of paper and put it on my cupboard in the kitchen where I would have to read it several times a day. This verse instructs us to "bear with each other," which clearly indicates that we are going to have challenges in our relationships. Some of us more than others.

Again, this does not mean that you endure abuse or mistreatment. Abuse is another category altogether, and it is important that you remove yourself and your children from abusive environments. Don't just hope it will go away; take action, because the long-term affects of abuse can be devastating. If you think you may be in an abusive situation, seek the help of a pastor, counselor, and community resources to help you decide how to proceed.

When we bear with one another, we recognize that we often bug each other and frustrate and hurt one another. We must remember that God gave us His grace. We must also extend that grace to one another in our relationships. It is prideful to hold a grudge, because each one of us is prone to disappoint others, say insensitive things, and neglect relationships. This doesn't mean that we actively pursue relationships that are harmful to us. It means that we let go of the grudge, we forgive, and we give them another chance because God has given us another chance.

Forgiving Ourselves

Clearly the problem is not always that we cannot forgive others, but that we cannot forgive ourselves. Our human nature wants to proclaim that we are innocent and it is because of the people around us who hurt us that we are seething with rage. We blame our anger on them or justify our own actions, saying that our anger is because of how they treated us. We often don't want to admit our own failures, and so we are unable to accept the fact that we also do hurtful things to others.

When we are unable to forgive ourselves or even see that we need to forgive ourselves, we have a tendency to do what psychologists call *projection*. Projection occurs when we cannot tolerate the traits that we dislike in ourselves, so we attribute those traits to others around us. For example: we blame others for being insensitive when really it is our own problem.

We have to take a stance of humility to admit that it is our own problem and not the problem of everyone around us. I like what our pastor, Greg Thompson, says when he is preaching about a topic that involves personal change. He reminds us to focus on ourselves and not think, "Oh, uncle so and so needs to hear this." That might be true, but it is important to recognize how it applies to us. We all project from time to time, and in its more severe forms, projection is a defense structure that can be very destructive to our relationships. It is destructive because when we are defensive rather than truthful, we sabotage trust, and we accuse others of the things we do. This is hurtful to the people we love.

Another consequence of not forgiving ourselves is low self-esteem. We spend our lives overcompensating for the mistakes we have made, and our relationships become unbalanced. We feel that we are indebted to others, and we are convinced we are not worth loving. This hinders our ability to be assertive and can lead to resentment and imbalance in our relationships, usually with ourselves on the bottom end. We are convinced we deserve to be treated poorly, and so we tolerate being treated that way—unable to forgive ourselves and, therefore, unable to stand up for ourselves in a way that is healthy.

Not forgiving ourselves also snubs God, because it communicates that His grace is not sufficient for us. It means that Jesus' suffering on the cross was not enough for us. It forsakes His love and His grace and mercy in our lives. Jesus didn't suffer and die on the cross so that we could continue to wallow in our sins and walk in shame. He suffered so we can hold our heads up in confidence, knowing that His grace *is* sufficient for us (see 2 Cor. 12:9)! He gives us His love and favor even though we don't deserve it. That fact gives us the freedom to forgive even ourselves when we don't live up to our own expectations. Isn't it comforting to know that His grace is sufficient for us, if we choose to accept it?

CHOOSE TO FORGIVE

We must choose to forgive ourselves and others. Forgiveness recognizes that a wrong has been done. It then offers or accepts an apology, and in response forgives or accepts forgiveness. We must make an active choice to forgive. Many of us don't want to struggle with it, so we prefer to pretend we are okay. I can attest that it doesn't always come automatically, but we need to be willing to press into forgiveness.

If you are struggling with forgiveness, ask people to pray for you, write key verses and post them in places you can see them daily. Ask God to help you. Actively participate in the process until you feel forgiveness taking hold and the anger dissipating. You will know when true forgiveness happens because you will feel more free, light, and relieved.

When the weed of un-forgiveness and anger is pulled from our lives, we are able to bear fruit again. Our spiritual growth is no longer hindered, and we are free to live in the present and not in the past. We can get back into alignment with God's plans for us and move in that direction without being weighted down with un-forgiveness. Doesn't that sound appealing? We may not be aware of how much un-forgiveness is holding us back until we are free from it.

REALIGNMENT

Recently I have been going to the chiropractor for chronic neck and back problems. I can now move my neck freely, without pain or restriction, for the first time in years. I am amazed at the free movement my neck has. Prior to this a friend had asked, "Are you okay? Your neck looks stiff." It felt normal to me because it had been stiff for many years. So I said, "Yes, I am fine." But now that my neck is free to move, I can look back and see how bad it was. The same is true for un-forgiveness. It brings us out of alignment with God's Holy Spirit and His will for our lives. It restricts our movement.

To further my point, my chiropractor told me about a man who had been blind in his right eye for 12 years. And when he went to get an adjustment from his chiropractor, his eyes started watering for about 45 minutes. Then his eyesight was restored. He was amazed that a spinal adjustment had restored his sight (*Telegraph Herald*). Sometimes when we receive a spiritual adjustment by submitting to God's Word, we are able to see more clearly. Choosing unforgiveness misaligns us spiritually. Choosing to forgive puts us back in alignment with His truth and His grace and enables us to grow and become who He has planned us to be. Make that choice today to forgive others and to forgive yourself.

POINTS TO CONSIDER: ANGER VS. FORGIVENESS

- Anger is often related to feelings of hurt, sadness, disappointment, or other emotions.
- If unchecked, anger can be destructive to our relationships, including our relationship with God.
- Forgiveness heals and allows room for God to intervene.

EXPLORATION QUESTIONS

1. Am I angry at someone? What about? Whom do I need to forgive?
2. Do I have trouble controlling my anger? Do I suppress unresolved anger?
3. How has Jesus forgiven me?
4. How can I surrender to God's command to forgive?
5. In what ways has unforgiveness held me back? What are the benefits for me if I choose forgiveness?

FOCUS VERSE

Therefore, as God's chosen people, holy and dearly loved, clothe yourselves with compassion, kindness, humility, gentleness and patience. Bear with each other and forgive whatever grievances you may have against one another. Forgive as the Lord forgave you. And over all these virtues put on love, which binds them all together in perfect unity.

—Colossians 3:12–14

117

Focus Prayer

Lord, I am sorry for not dealing with my anger well. Help me to learn how to handle anger in a way that is pleasing to You. Help me to forgive the people who have hurt me and whom I have anger towards. And help me to forgive myself. Thank You for forgiving me and giving Your grace. Help me to extend Your grace to others by Your strength. Help me also to forgive myself for the mistakes I make so that I can walk in your grace. In Jesus' name, amen.

CHAPTER 8

THE WEED OF DENIAL
VS.
THE FRUIT OF REPENTANCE

Denial—a state of mind marked by a refusal or an
inability to recognize and deal with a serious personal
problem.
—Encarta Dictionary

I Am Not in Denial...am I?

DENIAL IS A bit like walking on quicksand. With each
step further into denial, we get trapped deeper and
deeper into its pit. Those who get trapped in quicksand
don't realize that's where they are until it begins to pull them
down and they are stuck. The deeper we get into denial, the
more difficult it is to get out of. Denial holds us in its grip
and continues to pull us down without mercy. Eventually
it will choke the life out of us if we let it.

I read an article in *Readers Digest* about how rescuers
figured out how to get people out of quicksand before they
died of suffocation. After several failed attempts, the team
developed a long tube that could blast air underneath the victim to release him or her from the tight grip of the quicksand

119

while the team pulled the person out to safety. Nothing else worked. When being released from denial, often it requires a team. The air that gets blasted underneath to loosen the grip is repentance and truth. The team is accountability.

WHEN DENIAL IS EXPOSED

When denial begins to crack open, fear and grief often follow—the very emotions that have prevented you from going forward. It is critical to recognize that fear and grief will not destroy you, but whatever you are avoiding might. I remember a particular time when I finally took that needed step out of denial, I wept for hours and hours. I wept because it hurt to face myself and my choices and the loss of time I had invested in those choices.

However, at the same time, I also felt relief, because I was finally positioned to change. I was now being truthful with myself even though it hurt and would require some significant changes. I regretted not having taken the steps out of denial earlier. It came with the help of a trusted friend who confronted me head on with the truth about the situation and with a willingness on my part to finally admit that I needed to change my course.

What I did know is that I could trust the Lord and I could trust His leading, even if I was late in following it. The truth was that I needed to learn from the mistakes I had made. I felt hurt and confused, but at the same time relieved and hopeful that as I leaned into God He would heal me and teach me what I needed to learn if only I was willing.

THE POWER OF TRUTH IN HEALING

Truth—Accuracy in description or portrayal; honesty, sincerity, or integrity. Correspondence to fact or reality.
—Encarta Dictionary

120

Truth and truthfulness is a central component of living a complete life. God is very clear about the importance of truth in our walk with Him. Truth does several things, including: it protects us (see Ps. 40:11), and it brings us closer to God. "The LORD is near to all who call on him, to all who call on him in truth" (Ps. 145:18). It is also associated with the development of important character traits. "Buy the truth and do not sell it; get wisdom, discipline and understanding" (Prov. 23:23). Therefore, truth has value.

In addition, truth seeks God's favor, while the lack of truth forsakes it. "Yet we have not sought the favor of the LORD our God by turning from our sins and giving attention to your truth" (Dan. 9:13). In lacking truthfulness, there is a consequence: "The LORD did not hesitate to bring the disaster upon us, for the LORD our God is righteous in everything he does; yet we have not obeyed him" (Dan. 9:14). When we are in direct disobedience to God and are not truthful, we can experience adversity.

In addition, God desires truth. "Surely you desire truth in the inner parts; you teach me wisdom in the inmost place" (Ps. 51:6). Therefore, if we are willing, He will teach us the value of truth because He looks for the truth. "O LORD, do not your eyes look for truth?" (Jer. 5:3). The Lord searches for people who are truthful, and He will take notice when we are truthful or are not truthful. Truthfulness is associated with loyalty to God and His Word.

Jesus frequently prefaced statements with "I tell you the truth" and emphasized that knowing the truth "will set us free" (John 8:32). It also brings us into His light and bears fruit in our lives. "But whoever lives by the truth comes into the light, so that it may be seen plainly that what he has done has been done through God" (John 3:21).

Temptation to Avoid Truth

If truth is so important, why then are we tempted to change facts and muddle the truth to mask our true intentions? If we are honest with ourselves, we are all tempted to do this on a regular basis. We always have a choice to speak truthfully or to cloud over the truth with lies and misrepresentations. We need to be reminded that in "speaking the truth in love, we will in all things grow up into him who is the Head, that is, Christ. From him the whole body, joined and held together by every supporting ligament, grows and builds itself up in love, as each part does its work" (Eph. 4:15–16). The gospels urge us over and over to seek truth because we are connected to one another as the body of Christ, and therefore, our actions not only affect ourselves, but also others. When we lie it affects the whole body, and we fail to mature in our faith.

Some of us habitually minimize, distort, omit, or blatantly change facts. Others may do it from time to time. The result is the same; we wind up colluding with the enemy of our souls and harming ourselves and others. We are exhorted "not to lie to each other, since you have taken off your old self with its practices and have put on the new self, which is being renewed in knowledge in the image of its Creator" (Col. 3:9–10). Being truthful is a fruit of our faith in God.

Excuses

We may justify our actions by telling ourselves we are protecting ourselves or protecting someone we feel isn't ready to hear the truth. We decide through passivity that we are not willing to grow in our relationships, and so we live behind a mask. Sometimes we are participating fully in one or more addictions, so we lie to ourselves to minimize the apparent impact and postpone recovery.

Lying sometimes seems innocent, however, it is not neutral...it hands over power to the enemy who would love to destroy our lives. He is patient and will wait through a lifetime of denial and lies to see a life slowly disintegrate indiscriminately so that the individual fails to notice the depth of the impact until a tremendous amount of damage has been done. Therefore, being passive about this issue can cause serious harm over time—an addiction may progress, an affair may continue, marriage issues don't get addressed, children act out in anger, trust is damaged, and healing is postponed.

STAGNANT FAITH

Denial results in stagnancy in our growth and indicates a lack of trust in God to carry us through pain into positive changes (Ps. 55:19). In contrast, when we turn over our fear and our pain to God, He will sustain us and will help us through without allowing us to fall (see Ps. 55:22). Denial keeps us in the dark and hinders us from seeing the truth. Without truth we cannot see clearly. Our lives become confusing. We cannot trust others and we feel increasingly uncertain.

Facing the truth can be tremendously painful when denial has been protecting us from the pain of realizing how bad our situation has become or how abusive our relationship is or how deep our debt is. Truth can be a painful realization. We often aren't ready to do the work that is required to pursue change. Denial postpones recovery.

I know that when I was in an abusive relationship years ago, I was in profound denial about it. Denial meant I didn't have to change or make a decision. Once I moved out of denial, I felt a flood of painful emotions, from tremendous grief to anger at myself to sadness about wasted time and uncertainty about the future. I was scared and hopeful at the same time. I knew it would take a while to recover, but I also suddenly had clarity about what I needed to do. I needed my friends to be there for me, and I needed to press into God and His leading in my life.

Scripture says, "If you really change your ways and your actions and deal with each other justly, if you do not oppress the alien, the fatherless or the widow and do not shed innocent blood in this place, and if you do not follow other gods to your own harm, then I will let you live in this place, in the land I gave your forefathers for ever and ever" (Jer. 7:5–8). If we change our ways and stop believing a lie that may be our own denial, then God promises to be faithful and bring us to a more fruitful place in our lives. The "land" promised might be reduced debt, healthier relationships, restored health, freedom from addictions, or other beneficial outpourings of truth in our life. It may be a free conscience. For me it was healthier relationships.

Blessings in Truth

God wants to bless us, but when we are in a cloud of denial we cannot make the positive changes needed to position ourselves for His blessing. God's blessing resides only under the umbrella of truth. When we are truthful, we move from stagnancy, heartache, and separation from God to a position of blessing. "Blessed are they whose transgressions are forgiven, whose sins are covered. Blessed is the man whose sin the Lord will never count against him." (Rom. 4:7–8). We are blessed by God when we are honest about our mistakes, and He never holds it against us. Isn't that a wonderful relief?

THE IMPORTANCE OF HONESTY

Honesty means admitting that we are sinful and therefore we have a tendency to make selfish decisions, hurt others, deny God's leading, lie to ourselves, and lie to others. Yet, Scripture makes it clear that "if we claim to be without sin, we deceive ourselves and the truth is not in us" (1 John 1:8). We *minimize* the impact of our sin on ourselves and others. We brush it off and fail to recognize or admit its destructiveness in our lives and how it impacts others.

Being honest with ourselves is not enough; we also need to be honest with others. When we are deep in denial, we often are not just lying to ourselves, we are lying to others. We tell ourselves, "It's not that bad," or "It's not hurting anyone." Maybe we just postpone making changes and tell ourselves we will get to it tomorrow. We may have every intention of doing so, but we lack the resolve to put in the effort that is required. Possibly others are confronting you, and so you tell them that you plan to change with no intention of ever doing so. Whatever the source of your denial, it delays your growth like a weed hinders the growth of a plant.

HUMBLE ADMITTANCE

Yet, "if we confess our sins, he is faithful and just and will forgive us our sins and purify us from all unrighteousness" (1 John 1:9). Isn't that wonderful? All we have to do is admit that we have sinned and we are cleansed and forgiven. It is so simple and straightforward, yet we struggle to do it because of pride.

Humbly admitting our sins and shortcomings is critical to our relationship with God and our pursuit of a fruitful spiritual life. Regularly practicing the discipline of repentance is crucial to moving forward. "Repent, then, and turn to God, so that your sins may be wiped out, that times of refreshing may come from the Lord" (Acts 3:19).

Along with repentance comes refreshing. We are refreshed and enabled to grow. When we repent it is like a plant getting freshly watered and given fertilizer. The roots drink and the rest of the plant thrives and comes back to life. Similarly, we take in God's forgiveness and our hearts are cleansed, and then we are free to grow in faith with the sustaining power of God's grace and love. When I start to feel stagnant, I become aware that I haven't repented recently and then I must make time to spend with God in prayer and repentance. I feel a difference in my spirit immediately, and a heavy cloud is lifted off of me.

Sometimes I am astounded by how honest my children can be. I may ask my son directly, "Did you take that from your sister?" He sheepishly will say, "Yes, I did." Only now that he is getting a little bit older, he occasionally attempts to cover up his actions. Truthfully, I am more angered by his attempts to lie then by the action itself. If he tells me the truth, I address it and ask him to apologize to his sister. When he lies it becomes a character issue that is deeper and more important for me to address. Most of the time I know exactly what happened, but I ask him to tell me to give him a chance to be honest. God gives us chances to be honest. We need to take those opportunities while restoration is straightforward. When we cover it up we may develop a pattern and become insensitive to our conscience. Deeper lies creep in and our character changes.

WITHOUT REPENTANCE PRIDE GRIPS US

The lack of repentance is not benign, it is cancerous. It is a weed that severely hinders our spiritual growth. Without repentance we cannot change, without change we cannot break through the challenges we face. When we repent we are able to change habits that seem to have a hold on us. Repentance keeps us grounded in reality; it maintains our humility and is an antidote to pride. Without it our human, sinful nature and pride begin to take hold, and we move farther and farther from Him.

Many people who attend church regularly are full of pride and don't understand their need to repent. When I repent, the first thing I always ask forgiveness for is pride, because I know I have pride whether I want to admit it or not. That clears the air for me to see the other things I need to repent of—un-forgiveness, selfishness, idolatry, anger, complaining, insensitivity to others, fearfulness, and not trusting God. When we humbly admit we are sinful and prideful, then we allow room for the Holy Spirit to convict us. We can do this at any time and in any place. We do not just repent in church. Anytime the Holy Spirit brings conviction it is important to ask for forgiveness immediately. Don't wait for confession or the next service you happen to get to. The moment conviction comes, God's grace also comes to assist you in overcoming your habit, to clarify for you what you need to do and how you can do it.

CONVICTION CLARIFIES

Conviction feels clean because it gives room for us to heal and change. When I have been convicted and have confessed, I have felt the presence of the Holy Spirit helping me to change. Conviction occurs when the Holy Spirit pricks your conscience with His love for you and intolerance for sin that is harmful. God convicts so that we can be healed. He says "confess and be healed" (James 5:16). Confessing to others and to God that we have done wrong heals us. It doesn't leave us stranded or feeling guilty.

Conversely, guilt is often a negative emotion. We can feel guilty about many things, but unable to change. Guilt weighs us down and feels cruddy. Guilt shames us and makes us feel horrible about ourselves. Shame prevents us from moving forward and allowing our sins to come into the light. When shame overpowers us and the enemy convinces us that our sins are too shameful to confess, we must look to the truth in God's promise that "those who look to him are radiant; their faces are never covered with shame" (Ps. 34:5). He promises that He will not shame us, but He will help us and heal us and forgive us.

Conviction comes with love and compassion: "God's kindness leads you toward repentance" (Rom. 2:4). We confess because we know that we are loved and we are assured that the Lord is caring toward us. God's love and compassion provide the safety we need to repent as often as we need, because when we repent, we receive God's mercy and forgiveness. There is no greater freedom than the feeling of forgiveness.

We need to be childlike in our faith. Children are so open and honest. Possibly this is why Jesus said, "I tell you the truth, unless you change and become like little children, you will never enter the kingdom of heaven. Therefore, whoever humbles himself like this child is the greatest in the kingdom of heaven" (Matt. 18: 3, 4). Imitating how open and honest children are helps us to work toward that type of childlike faith and truthfulness. The benefits are spiritual growth, healing, restoration, and the hope of heaven.

POSITIONED FOR BLESSING

I don't know about you, but I want to be in a position to receive blessings from the Lord. I have experienced His blessings first hand, and I desire to continue to be able to encounter the Lord's work in my life. His work far surpasses my own. I have learned that I can trust Him. If repentance allows God's mercy, forgiveness, and blessings to enter into my life, then I will not hesitate to repent when I am convicted. Even when I know that I have acted out of my human nature and have not pleased the Lord with my actions or my words, I desire not to let my actions become a wedge in my relationship with the Lord. I want to feel cleansed and whole and pursued by my Maker to move forward in my life, rather then being stuck in a cesspool of deception, pride, and denial of the truth.

God has given us a promise that "he who conceals his sins does not prosper, but whoever confesses and renounces them finds mercy" (Prov. 28:13). Being close to the Lord is a wonderful, intimate feeling. I enjoy His presence. When we are truthful and when we confess our shortcomings we are able to fully enjoy His presence in our life without hindrances bogging us down.

POINTS TO CONSIDER: DENIAL VS. REPENTANCE

- Denial is common when we are not ready or willing to face a personal problem.
- Truthfulness helps us to address things properly and restores relationship.
- When we repent, God meets us with love and mercy and He helps us to change.

EXPLORATION QUESTIONS

1. Am I in denial? In what areas?
2. What drives my denial?
3. How can I begin to move out of denial and into truth?

4. What do I need to repent of? What prevents me from taking this step?
5. How can I allow repentance to heal me from things that hold me back?

Focus Verse

If we claim to be without sin, we deceive ourselves and the truth is not in us. If we confess our sins, he is faithful and just and will forgive us our sins and purify us from all unrighteousness. If we claim we have not sinned, we make him out to be a liar and his word has no place in our lives.

—1 John 1:8–10

Focus Prayer

Lord, help me to move out of denial. Lord, forgive me for not being honest with myself and others. I pray for the strength to be truthful with You and trust Your healing process in my heart. I repent of pride and dishonesty and pray for Your grace to heal me. In Jesus' name, amen.

CHAPTER 9

THE WEED OF
COMPLAINING
VS.
THE FRUIT OF GRATITUDE

Give thanks to the LORD, for he is good; His love endures
forever.

—1 Chronicles 16:34

WOW IS THIS is a hard one for me. It's not that I have
a hard time saying thank you. I do it all the time.
My friends and family even tease me for sending too many
thank you notes for everything under the sun. I just can't
help myself. However, I have a lot of difficulty remaining
free from complaining. I know that complaining is caustic,
and I have been convicted over and over about it. I repent
often. Yet, I still slip into it. This is where I can relate to the
apostle Paul when he says, "For what I want to do I do not
do, but what I hate I do" (Rom. 7:15), since even though I
don't want to complain, I still tend to do it.

As I observe my own complaining behavior, I realize
that I have more than one way of doing it. I have become
very creative in my efforts to complain, even if I am not
intentionally setting out to do so. First there is the direct

complaint, "I'm cold," or "We never go out to movies anymore." Then there is the indirect complaint made in casual conversation where I throw in a random comment about something that I am not entirely pleased about and keep talking as if I am not really complaining. Do you know what I am talking about? Have you done this before? I know some of you know exactly what I am talking about.

One example of indirect complaining that I say is, "Our house is small so we have to store our things in the garage." Interpreted this means, "I want a bigger house." This seems to be just a benign, factual statement, but in my heart, it is complaining. I desire a bigger house. The complaint seems harmless, but it sets me back on a focus that is negative rather than positive. The truth is that I can see God's wisdom in keeping us in our current home. I am a packrat and have been taught to keep everything and to place sentimental value on all of it. When my husband and I first married, I had stored up tons of stuff that I never used. I had tremendous guilt in even considering throwing it out or giving it away. Having a home with limited storage has forced me to start purging (much to my husband's relief), which has been a terrifically freeing experience. I may have sniffled a little when I got rid of my ratty old college sweatshirt, but I really don't miss it.

DEEPER PROBLEM

Complaining causes us to focus on the negative and hinders us from enjoying the positive. The more often we complain, the more of a habit it becomes. It can also lead to a deeper problem of depression because we start to perceive the world around us very negatively. Whether we complain directly, indirectly, or both, it chips away at our contentment and eats away at our joy. It creates a general mood of dissatisfaction that begins to pervade every aspect of our lives. It affects how we feel, how we interact with others, and what we hope for and strive to attain in our life.

When we complain, we forget that God is taking care of us, and we begin to lack hope for the future. Yes, life is hard, and yes, we can get hurt by others, and clearly things often don't go our way. However, we have a loving God who cares for us and will sustain us and who gives us the hope of heaven.

GRATEFULNESS

The weed killer for complaining is gratefulness. When I find myself complaining, I try to shift gears to thankfulness for all God has given to me. I don't always feel grateful when I thank the Lord for His blessings. Often I would rather complain and feel sorry for myself. I choose to thank Him because I know that I don't deserve what I have. He blesses me through His mercy and grace because He loves me. The more thankful I am, the more I begin to enjoy what I have.

As I start to focus on the positives rather than the negatives, joy begins to replace the depression. An internal shift takes place over time, and it becomes easier to focus on good things in our lives, both big and small. It can be as simple as *Thank you God for running water,* or *Thank you for the hope of heaven.*

CONSTANT STRUGGLE

After attempting to break myself of this habit over the years and continuing to fail even with frequent repentance, I still find that complaining and grumbling creeps back into my attitude. It is something that nearly always needs to be kept in check. Because of this, it seems to me that it is definitely a part of our sinful nature to complain and whine and see what we don't have and what others do have. For me all it takes is one trip to the store. I might be winning the battle of contentment and then I need to go to a store to pick up a gift for someone. Immediately, I am aware of how much I don't have and what I could have, and I start to feel my inner spirit warring against my greed. I walk out of the store feeling discontented and desiring more.

Often we begin to rationalize—*I work hard. I live in a free country. I have a right to keep up with the latest fashion trend. I want more. Everybody else seems to be able to have all these things except for me.* Whine, whine, whine, and the discontentment we feel begins to seep into other areas of our lives.

Once I let complaining loose and allow it to have a voice in my spirit, it pervades my thoughts—*I should be able to landscape the front of my house. I should have a new car. I should have a new dining room table and chairs. I should be able to buy what I want.* And the list goes on. Fortunately, with some practice, I have learned to rein it in. And rein it in we must. If we allow complaining to take root in our hearts, it embitters us and generates an undercurrent of misery. There will always be something to complain about.

In today's culture we often use the word "deserve" to justify our wants and our complaining. We tell each other that we deserve certain things. Sales slogans emphasize that we deserve their product or deserve a better life. But the Scriptures explain that by God's grace we are spared what we really deserve. "He does not treat us as our sins deserve or repay us according to our iniquities" (Ps. 103:10). For that we ought to be thankful.

UNDERESTIMATION

The thing is that we underestimate complaining. It is one of those weeds that doesn't seem so harmful. It might even have a flower top to disguise it. It is a little bothersome, but if we don't get to it right away, then it's okay. We can always deal with it later. The truth is that it is a momentous problem and should be dealt with immediately. God does not take grumbling lightly and described complaining as wickedness and rebellion against Him:

> The LORD replied, "I have forgiven them, as you asked. Nevertheless, as surely as I live and as surely as the glory of the LORD fills the whole earth, not one of the men who saw my glory and the miraculous signs I performed in Egypt and in the desert but who disobeyed me and tested me ten times—not one of them will ever see the land I promised on oath to their forefathers. No one who has treated me with contempt will ever see it. But because my servant Caleb has a different spirit and follows me wholeheartedly, I will bring him into the land he went to, and his descendants will inherit it…" The LORD said to Moses and Aaron: "How long will this wicked community grumble against me?"
> —Numbers 14:20–27

When we complain about what we don't have, we end up robbing ourselves of the blessings God intends to give us for our faithfulness to Him. He wants to bring us into our personal promised land, but as long as we complain and grumble, we forfeit our chance to receive it. God may postpone the blessings until He knows we can handle them without losing perspective.

Much as a toddler wants what they want "now," we also have difficulty waiting on God. When we ask a child to "wait," he or she will assume we are saying "no" or he or she is just unwilling to wait. Sometimes before I let my kids know they can have something, I make sure they have cleaned up their messes. I ask them, "Are your toys put away? Did you make your bed? Have you completed your responsibilities? If so, then yes, you can have a chocolate chip cookie," although I often give it to them just because I love them.

GOD GIVES GOOD GIFTS

God also gives good gifts to us just because He loves us. He provides for our needs and cares for us. It is His desire to bless us. He wants us to ask Him for what we need and explains, "Which of you, if his son asks for bread, will give him a stone? Or if he asks for a fish, will give him a snake? If you, then, though you are evil, know how to give good gifts to your children, how much more will your Father in heaven give good gifts to those who ask him" (Matt. 7:9–11). He knows how to give good gifts better than anyone we know, and He encourages us to ask Him for them.

ACCORDING TO HIS WILL

Sometimes we are running into attitude problems because we fail to even ask God. We compartmentalize our wants and feel selfish for asking God for things. Then, instead of asking, we either deny ourselves or we seek after the blessings on our own. Yet the Lord is clear that He wants to give good gifts to His followers if we ask Him (Matt. 7:7; Matt. 18:19; Matt. 21:22). He might say, "Wait, have you cleaned up your messes? Have you surrendered to me? Are you in alignment with my will?" We might have to make some adjustments and do our part. He says if we ask for anything according to His will, He will give it to us! "I tell you the truth, my Father will give you whatever you ask in my name. Until now you have not asked for anything in my name. Ask and you will receive, and your joy will be complete" (John 16:23–24).

If we ask in His name, meaning in alignment with His will, His character, and His blessings, He says that He will give it to us. I have often been surprised by the Lord's generosity to me. I don't know why this would surprise me, that a loving God would answer my little prayers. I do know that as I have continued to lean into Him and seek Him and follow His will, He has blessed me with many things and aspects of life that I have enjoyed.

Sometimes my requests weren't answered immediately. I had to wait a while. Other times my requests were answered right away. There were times that I didn't receive what I prayed for until I had completely surrendered it to God and stopped wanting it. There were times that specifics were given, such as a plan for me to proceed in a certain direction in my life. What is important is to always be in a stance of learning and gratitude for what you do have. Gratitude fills the heart with joy in all circumstances. When we are grateful, then we are happy in our souls, even if not in our circumstances.

CHOOSE GRATITUDE

Much of life is a challenge, and often there is plenty to complain about. To think that we will stop complaining once our life is better is a false belief. There will always be something to complain about. Complaining is a habit, and a mighty stubborn one I might add, but it is something we must choose to put aside. We choose gratitude moment by moment in our daily lives and use it to subdue the nature of the flesh that will complain bitterly if given the freedom to do so. Choosing to refrain from complaining purifies us and sets us apart to glorify God. "Do everything without complaining or arguing, so that you may become blameless and pure, children of God without fault in a crooked and depraved generation, in which you shine like stars in the universe" (Phil. 2:14–15).

We not only are grateful to God, but also to each other. It is important to say thanks to others for work they do, gifts they give, time they spend, prayers and support they extend. It communicates a genuine love in community to be grateful for the things that we do in service to one another. Having a grateful heart helps us keep perspective on God's loving care for us and on our place in the world around us. It reminds us that there are many who are suffering more than we are, and that life has more meaning to it than whether or not we are comfortable all of the time.

FRUIT OF GRATITUDE

The fruit of gratitude is joy in the midst of circumstances and peace in the midst of trials. When we are grateful, we get perspective that life really is about relationships with God and with people. It is about sharing God's love with others. Gratitude doesn't guarantee that we will always have everything we want or that we will be comfortable. It *does* help us to remember God's goodness and His grace, and it recognizes that it is God who takes care of us.

I was struck by the family in the movie *Hotel Rwanda*, in which people faced unthinkable horrors and losses. I noticed that the husband and hotel manager mentioned that he had taken the time to thank God for his family everyday and continued to do so in the middle of the tremendous hardship they faced as a family and culture. I wondered if the gratitude he had for his family was part of the reason

God used him to be a blessing and a source of strength for many others during the crisis. He wasn't spared heartache and grief, but his family was protected, and He was used by God to spare the lives of many people and families. His attitude of gratefulness helped him overcome even the most adverse circumstances.

THE HEART OF CHILDREN

Because children are so transparent, we can use the beautiful hearts of children as an example of gratitude. When I tuck my son in at night and ask him what he wants to thank God for, he thanks God for his bed, his toys, the curtains, a warm house, the planets and stars, his socks and shoes, and my favorite one is when he thanks God for "everything that He has made." In using a child's model for prayer, we ought to take the time to thank God for our clothes, our food, and the fact that we can see, for heat in our homes, and all of the things that we often take for granted. Every day I thank God for the house we live in, and I enjoy our home more and more. When we thank God for these things, we become filled with joy and are less focused on what we don't have and more focused on what we do have and on what is truly important—relationships with God and with each other.

POINTS TO CONSIDER: COMPLAINING VS. GRATITUDE

- Complaining hinders us from enjoying life and breeds discontentment.
- Gratitude helps us to focus on the good things in our lives and enables us to receive God's blessings.
- Gratitude replaces discontentment with joy.

EXPLORATION QUESTIONS

1. What do I complain about?
2. How does complaining affect my life negatively?
3. What do I have to be grateful about?
4. What prevents me from having a grateful attitude?
5. How can I be more deliberate about having an attitude of gratefulness in my life?

FOCUS VERSE

Let the peace of Christ rule in your hearts, since as members of one body you were called to peace. And be thankful. Let the word of Christ dwell in you richly as you teach and admonish one another with all wisdom, and as you sing psalms, hymns, and spiritual songs with gratitude in your hearts to God. And whatever you do, whether in word or deed, do it all in the name of the Lord Jesus, giving thanks to God the Father through him.

—Colossians 3:15–17

FOCUS PRAYER

Lord, forgive me for complaining and for lacking a spirit of gratitude for all that You have given to me. Even when times are hard and things seem against me, I have much to be thankful for. I am so glad that You care for me as much as you do. Please supply my needs and show me how to follow Your will for my life. Thank You for all of Your many blessings including _____

_____ in Jesus' name, amen.

CHAPTER 10

THE WEED OF RELIGIOUSNESS VS. THE FRUIT OF AUTHENTICITY

WHAT IS RELIGIOUSNESS? Religiousness is ritual without faith. It is going through the motions of church without true relationship with God. It is empty and void of love for God and relies on appearing to do all of the right things without truly believing the Bible or having a relationship with Jesus.

NOXIOUS WEEDS

Most weeds are *invasive,* and in that they are problematic because they grow where they are not wanted. However, *noxious* weeds are even more overpowering than other types of weeds. These weeds are designated by local or national governments as "noxious" because they cause profound injury to public health, livestock, agriculture, wildlife refuges, and personal property. Noxious weeds can permanently damage property, making it dormant and irreversibly unproductive. They have been known to do several types of damage, including completely destroying wildlife habitats, and that displaces wildlife, including endangered species.

They disrupt migratory bird patterns and significantly decrease the health of eco-systems, resulting in millions of dollars of damage for which the government must pay.

In the spiritual realm, *religiousness* is a noxious weed. Religiousness without faith can affect entire church communities, organizations, and ministries, and affect the people in their care. Religiousness is prevalent within the church. Unfortunately, it is easy to develop a religious attitude within our Christian community.

GOING THROUGH THE MOTIONS

I remember attending a church where the pastors wore rich dark green robes and the choir wore robes and everyone dressed in formal attire for church. The service itself was pleasant, and the hymns that the choir sang were well rehearsed and beautiful. I enjoyed the sermons, yet I remember feeling a bit detached from it all. I was aware that I needed to make sure that I looked good, at least on the outside. We all smiled a lot and said hello. People chatted in the hallways and had coffee. We put on a persona that all was well and we were happy.

It felt a bit as if we were going through the motions of church without really connecting deeply with one another or with God. That doesn't mean there wasn't genuine connection or relationship there. People did have faith in God, but it didn't feel fully honest to me. I may have smiled a lot at church and had my dress and nylons and shoes coordinated, but on the inside I was hurting, and I wondered if anyone was aware of my pain or really knew who I was. It felt superficial.

I do remember listening to the sermons and growing in my faith there, but I still hungered for more. I felt that I was still getting milk when what I needed was solid food.

"Anyone who lives on milk, being still an infant, is not acquainted with the teaching about righteousness. But solid food is for the mature, who by constant use have trained themselves to distinguish good from evil" (Heb. 5:13–14). I asked God to lead me to a church where I would experience more of His presence, solid teaching, and more meaningful relationships.

AUTHENTIC CHURCH COMMUNITY

Astoundingly, when He led me to a church where people dressed casually, and I saw a wide range of people with a wide range of backgrounds and life experiences, I knew I was in a place where I could grow. The pretense was gone, and there were real people who truly wanted to know Jesus. There were also many different cultures and ethnic backgrounds represented at the church, and they all came together to worship God in the same place. I felt at home there.

What really blew me away was when, after a life-changing sermon, people would assemble at the front of the church to kneel or to stand and pray and receive prayer from a team of "pray-ers." People would begin to weep, and the Kleenex was always on hand to offer to people who were soaking in prayer. The presence of the Holy Spirit was tangible. Healing and spiritual growth was happening, and people were not afraid to show it.

Knowing that I needed prayer, I eagerly went for prayer week after week. I often wept and people prayed for me and quoted Scripture verses to me and truly seemed to understand me, even though they didn't know me. I began to heal in my heart. I could feel a tangible change in me that I could not fully describe, except that I knew I had encountered the presence of the Holy Spirit who was healing my hurting heart. I was surrounded by people who loved the Lord deeply and who were fervently growing in their relationship with Jesus. I loved being there, because for the first time in my life I could really be myself in church.

In community we encouraged each other and supported one another. We laughed, cried, quoted Scripture to each other, and prayed for one another. We helped each other move and made meals for those who were sick or who had just had a baby. We went to the area nursing home and prayed for the elderly together, and we served at the local soup kitchen. It felt good to serve one another this way.

DON'T GIVE UP ON CHURCH

Another unfortunate consequence of religiousness without authenticity is that some people will give up on the church altogether, yet we are encouraged not to "give up meeting together, as some are in the habit of doing, but let us encourage one another—and all the more as you see the Day approaching" (Heb. 10:25). If you don't feel at home in the church where you are worshiping, ask God to lead you to a new church home, or begin to pray for your church home, asking God to restore authentic faith. Churches are not perfect, and you won't find the perfect church, but seek to be where people can be themselves, and where God's Word is being taught.

When people give up on church and are quick to find faults within the community, it is easy to become isolated and vulnerable. When you aren't connected and start to face hard times, greater levels of discouragement can set in. Community is critical for sustaining our faith during hardship and the challenges of life. There is no such thing as a perfect church. All churches will have some faults.

MINISTER TO ONE ANOTHER

It was such a relief to me to find a church home where I could be myself, I could laugh and have conversation with my friends one moment and the next be praying fervent prayers that ministered healing in deep areas of hurt. It wouldn't faze us to sob in front of one another. We would just grab some Kleenex and keep praying. Then later we would say, "Let's go get lunch." We all seemed to understand that we each had something to work through to bring us closer to God, and so we easily gave one another that opportunity. There was a profound lack of a religiosity that could have hindered that process.

The most significant component was that the people there did not display an attitude that they were "fine" and didn't need help. And there was also a lack of judgment towards those who obviously weren't "fine." I noticed that people felt amazingly comfortable sharing their struggles with one another, and I began to feel at ease knowing that I had my own struggles. We struggled together, taking turns ministering to others and being ministered to. It felt as if the church was living out the New Testament admonishment to, "Let the word of Christ dwell in you richly as you teach and admonish one another with all wisdom" (Col. 3:16).

GENUINE FLAVOR

Reaching for some chocolate syrup, I looked at a label, and on the front of the product saw in bold letter the words "Genuine Flavor." I reviewed the ingredients and found that the "genuine ingredient" was only one of several listed on the back, along with many that were not healthy, such as high fructose corn syrup. In some ways this is what religiousness is—a lot of false ingredients—arrogance, pride, intellectualism, philosophy, materialism—for example, thrown in with the genuine ingredient to give the appearance that it is all "genuine." We participate in it without realizing we are consuming an unhealthy, tampered-with product that has a false appeal to it.

Currently the trend is to return to healthier and more wholesome food products, since studies reveal that altered products are causing a wide range of physical health problems. Some of these health problems are life-threatening. We strip products such as whole grain rice and wheat of their most beneficial properties, and then throw back in some vitamins. But people are increasingly at risk for heart attacks, high blood pressure, and other health problems as a result of these practices.

In the same way, when we alter the pure ingredients of spiritual worship we start to experience spiritual health problems. When we participate in false worship practices, void of the presence of the Holy Spirit, our soul is in jeopardy. Our hearts become distant from the Lord, and we may not even realize it, but we experience a deadening in our spirits, or even in our churches. I have walked into churches where there was a distinct lack of the presence of the Holy Spirit. People were doing what they thought they ought to do, but the presence of the Lord was lacking.

Jesus warned of the danger of tampering with true worship. "They worship me in vain; their teachings are but rules taught by men" (Matt. 15:9) Truthfully, I don't want to worship in vain. It is a waste of time and a concern for my spiritual well-being. I want to participate in worship that is genuine.

True Worship

True worship has only one main ingredient that Jesus stated emphatically: "Worship the Lord your God and serve him only" (Luke 4:8). When we begin to worship other things, and make the ritual of worship our idol, we add unhealthy ingredients that begin to cause spiritual health problems. Scripture warns against false worship more than once:

> Since you died with Christ to the basic principles of this world, why, as though you still belonged to it, do you submit to its rules: "Do not handle! Do not taste! Do not touch!"? These are all destined to perish with use, because they are based on human commands and teachings. Such regulations indeed have an appearance of wisdom, with their self-imposed worship, their false humility and their harsh treatment of the body, but they lack any value in restraining sensual indulgence.
>
> —Colossians 2:20–23

We can follow all of the rules that might be placed on us—dress up, smile, go to confession, don't dance, say your recited prayers, go to church every Sunday—and it can all be empty and void of the one and only true ingredient—relationship with the Lord.

In our flesh, we are prone to complicate things. True worship is simple—faith in the living God and relationship with Him through the power of the Holy Spirit. When we pull out that essential ingredient and add rules and regulations that we think "enrich" our worship experience, we mistakenly turn our focus to things that do not matter. We can do everything right—not lie, give to the poor, memorize verses—but it is spiritually meaningless if it is not saturated with true faith, because "without faith it is impossible to please God" (Heb. 11:6). When we are focused on having faith, we will desire to "live a life worthy of the calling we (you) have received" (Eph. 4:1). Our actions will become the fruit of our faith.

WARNINGS

To further understand what we need to strive for, it is important to understand what to refrain from. We take an honest look at how the Lord feels about religiousness without faith. In the Old Testament, the Lord states through His prophets, "I hate, I despise your religious feasts; I cannot stand your assemblies" (Amos 5:21). Those are strong negative words and shouldn't be taken lightly.

The Lord urges true worship. "Yet a time is coming and has now come when the true worshipers will worship the Father in spirit and truth, for they are the kind of worshipers the Father seeks. God is spirit, and his worshipers must worship in spirit and in truth" (John 4:23). He doesn't look for religious people. Instead He looks for those who worship in *spirit and truth,* because He wants a real connection with us. This also means that anyone can have access to relationship with God—poor or wealthy, old or young, trendy or sloppy, educated or uneducated—as long as you have a genuine heart for God.

He desires honest spirituality, where our spirits yield to Him and we are true to our faith in Him, as opposed to piousness where we appear to serve God yet are disconnected from relationship with God. In Isaiah, "the Lord says: 'These people come near to me with their mouth and honor me with their lips, but their hearts are far from me. Their worship of me is made up only of rules taught by men'" (Isa. 29:13). This can happen in varying degrees. You might think that you don't have this problem. Yet, I ask that you look deeper into your heart. If you are honest with yourself, you will admit that this is a daily struggle. We are always at war with our flesh and must seek the Lord to surrender our flesh to Him. Has your church life become a mere ritual? Have you become detached from your faith?

HUMAN NATURE

Our human nature likes rules, and we like to complicate things because we mistakenly think it makes life easier for us. In the short run it does. If we know what to expect and how to do it, we feel competent and capable. However, when we surrender our flesh to God and trust His ways, we are pulled out of our comfort zone every time. Trusting the Lord's plan for your life will challenge you deeply, yet those who choose to follow Jesus will find it is very rewarding. When we are authentic in our relationship with Him, we will bear fruit in our lives that we otherwise never could produce, even in our best effort.

Most of us would prefer comfort. Our earthly rules give us a false sense of comfort, but they can be truly toxic to the soul, because we are all vulnerable to placing rules above our true worship of God. Once we do that, the rules and ritual become an idol, and we are no longer in authentic relationship with Him.

NO ONE CAN BOAST

This affects not only how we conduct ourselves, but also how we feel when someone else doesn't follow protocol. We often become uneasy or even angry, we feel we must bring them back into the structure of our religion but fail to introduce them to the source of life—Jesus. I don't know about you, but I do not want to be a part of a religion of rules that leads to arrogance. God says that He does not allow us to base our faith on rules and spiritual accomplishments so that none of us can pride ourselves on our status with God.

Brothers, think of what you were when you were called. Not many of you were wise by human standards; not many were influential; not many were of noble birth. But God chose the foolish things of the world to shame the wise; God chose the weak things of the world to shame the strong. He chose the lowly things of this world and the despised things—and the things that are not—to nullify the things that are, so that no one may boast before him.

—1 Corinthians 1:26–29

Rules often lead to arrogance, which is not an option when following Jesus since He is clear in Scripture that we need to be realistic about who we really are and not rely on status or accomplishments. "For by the grace given me I say to every one of you: Do not think of yourself more highly than you ought, but rather think of yourself with sober judgment, in accordance with the measure of faith God has given you" (Rom. 12:3).

We must rely, not on accomplishments, but on faith. In faith we soak up God's love and presence, and we no longer need to take pride in our spiritual accomplishments because we realize that we are very much in need of God's grace.

PRIDE

I used to pride myself on the fact that I didn't party in high-school or college and that I worked hard to keep my relationships pure. I was proud that I didn't smoke or drink or use certain swear words. I was proud that I didn't watch certain shows because they were distasteful and promoted sexual immorality. God has graciously shown me that my prideful attitude is just as sinful as the sins I took pride in avoiding. My attitude of arrogance that I followed the rules was distasteful to God and bore a spirit of religion that God was not pleased with. Thankfully, I have repented of that attitude and try to keep it in check when it rises up in me.

150

I know that I am only saved by the grace of God and not by my own effort. I thank the Lord for that everyday.

A life-changing sermon I heard about focused on the older brother in the parable of the prodigal son. So often we focus on the prodigal son and forget to learn from the older brother's attitude and the father's response to him. Because the older brother took pride in his loyal and honorable actions toward his father, he felt he should get extra credit for it. He pouted in anger when his wayward brother returned and received back his inheritance in full and had a party thrown for him by his father. The older, faithful brother's arrogance needed to be corrected. So often, those of us who have walked the narrow path for any length of time can begin to take pride in our ability not to participate in obvious sinful practices, yet we fail to recognize our pride is also sinful.

SEEK HIM

We must refrain from holding an attitude of being "better than" because it is void of God's grace and mercy. God loves to extend mercy to those who know they need it. God says, "He rewards those who earnestly seek him" (Heb. 11:6). That is what is the most important to Him. When we seek Him with all of our hearts, we are engaging in true worship that is authentic and real. That is what He desires from us. God asks us to do simple and practical things as we practice our authentic faith. "Rejoice with those who rejoice; mourn with those who mourn. Live in harmony with one another. Do not be proud, but be willing to associate with people of low position. Do not be conceited" (Rom. 12:15–16). We must be authentic, which means that we are genuine and that we relate to others based on their real needs and that

151

we keep in mind we are all equally loved and valued by God, no matter what it is we are going through.

Let's confess our inclination to depend on rules to change our hearts and instead seek authentic worship of God. As we seek Him, we recognize He may pull us beyond our comfort level. He may even ask us to do things that others don't understand or aren't in agreement with. Are you willing to trust Him and worship Him in Spirit and truth?

OUT OF YOUR COMFORT ZONE

There have been times in my life when God called me to make decision without the support of others around me, because it didn't fit their structure of religion. It didn't make sense in the natural, but made perfect sense in alignment with a loving God who took my hand and led me in His plans for me. Our very lives are worship.

> Therefore, I urge you, brothers, in view of God's mercy, to offer your bodies as living sacrifices, holy and pleasing to God—this is your spiritual act of worship. Do not conform any longer to the pattern of this world, but be transformed by the renewing of your mind. Then you will be able to test and approve what God's will is—his good, pleasing and perfect will.
> —Romans 12:1–2

Only if we seek God with our hearts can we discover His will—not by following rules or earthly conventions. God will break through the walls of our religion box, lend His loving hand to help us out, and ask us to follow Him. It often doesn't make sense when we rely only on earthly structures. When God calls us beyond that structure is when we stand at the crossroads of true worship and sticking with religion. Can you step out of your area of comfort and your conventions? Is God asking you to lay them aside to follow Him?

Often when we are in disobedience to God, it is not intentional. It is because He calls us out of our norms and the status quo of religion and asks us to trust our authentic relationship with Him. When His will doesn't fit our expectations, we falter. We hesitate and go back under our comfort blanket of structured religion because we are afraid of the unknowns that exist beyond the organization of our religion. True worshippers follow Jesus, not rules, and He may take you to some unexpected places.

POINTS TO CONSIDER: RELIGIOUSNESS VS. AUTHENTICITY

- Religiousness is going to church and participating in ritual without true faith in God.
- God desires an authentic relationship with you.
- When we follow Jesus, He leads us by His love and grace and not by rules.

EXPLORATION QUESTIONS

1. Am I religious? Do I carry pride along with religiousness?
2. What drives my religious attitude? How does this affect my actions?
3. How can I be more authentic in my relationship with God?
4. How can I be more authentic in my relationships with others?
5. What is the benefit to experiencing authentic relationships with God and others?

FOCUS VERSE

If anyone considers himself religious and yet does not keep a tight rein on his tongue, he deceives himself and his religion is worthless. Religion that God our Father accepts as pure and faultless is this: to look after orphans and widows in their distress and to keep oneself from being polluted by the world.

—James 1:26–27

FOCUS PRAYER

Lord, forgive me for having a religious spirit and seeking after an external appearance of having it all together. Help me seek after an authentic relationship with You, and help me to worship in spirit and in truth. May I seek to be honest in my relationships with others. Forgive me for taking pride in religiousness rather than seeking true worship and true relationship with You. In Jesus' name, amen.

CHAPTER 11

THE WEED OF SELFISHNESS VS. THE FRUIT OF GIVING

THE NEXT BEST THING

ALL AROUND US we are bombarded by messages that are intended to convince us we need more things: bigger things, more attractive things. How often do we see commercials that play on our desires for fashion, new technology, and fully-loaded cars? Even children are enticed by commercials for new toys while they watch their favorite TV show. As a society, we have bought into the concept that we need to keep up with the latest trends. We want people to notice how well we are doing, and we don't want to miss out on anything that is out there for us to have or enjoy.

Our pastor at the Evanston Vineyard, Steve Nicholson, once preached a sermon on "The God of The Next Best Thing." He described the culture of needing the most recent and most extravagant gadget, car, or thing. We seek after the next gadget to hit the market, yet, once we possess it, we are left emotionally empty. Then we wait eagerly for the next upgrade to taunt us into purchasing it, and we are left feeling empty inside and waiting for the next thing to come along. For women, it may be the next shoe style, purse, or clothing trend. Truthfully, it doesn't satisfy our hearts to have more. It is only momentary, and it is not spiritually or emotionally satisfying. We need to be careful about putting too much emphasis on things. Seeking after things is an ongoing cycle that will never fill the void in our hearts.

Many of us have a compulsion to shop and buy. It would be easy to assume it is mostly women, but men also are compelled to shop for the things that interest them—gadgets, big screen TVs, golf clubs, to name a few. Many of us have experienced what is called "buyers remorse," which occurs fairly soon after a purchase and when we realize that it didn't satisfy us as deeply as we thought it would. We realize that the money could have been used more wisely. What compels us to purchase things we don't need and then feel remorse afterwards?

THE CONTROL FACTOR

One reason we purchase things is that it gives us a sense of control. When our life feels out of control, and we are experiencing a wide range of emotions and fears, it feels good to have a distraction, even if it is for just a moment. Being able to follow a routine of searching for, deciding on, and then completing the purchase gives us a temporary sense of control, whether it is a good decision or not. Researchers have even found that shopping raises the "feel-good" neuro-chemicals in our brain, which strongly reinforces the chances we will continue the behavior. We feel better when we shop, at least we feel better temporarily. Some are able to keep this in moderation, but for others it can become a compulsion that we struggle to resist.

When we do this, we self-medicate our anxieties, our losses, and our hurts with the feeling of control and purchase power. With a lack of healthy boundaries and a feeling that our lives are disorganized, we search for ways to bring a sense of control into our lives. If we feel inadequate, we look to things to fill us up, and at least by the world's standards we are seemingly adequate when we have wealth. Temporarily, a purchase feels good and restores a false sense of order to our lives.

When it becomes our focus to attain wealth, it can drive us to pursue a career to support our desire for more or can lead to poor financial decisions or to credit card debt. Many are successful business men and women and find it enjoyable to have wealth. The wealthy enjoy prestige, delicious meals at fancy restaurants, fashion, and nice cars. From a worldly perspective, it is enticing to strive for and attain wealth. Just turn on the TV or peruse the magazine rack, and we can observe how the wealthy are enjoying their fortunes. On the surface it looks thoroughly appealing.

However, spiritually, we are warned against such endeavors. "Do not wear yourself out to get rich; have the wisdom to show restraint" (Prov. 23:4). Seeking after riches is exhausting and is only temporary. "Cast but a glance at riches, and they are gone, for they will surely sprout wings and fly off to the sky like an eagle" (Prov. 23:5). Some lose their fortunes by living a life of excess.

Desiring Money Changes our Character

In addition, our focus on the accumulation of things changes our character. Our focus becomes self-centered, and we may cease to care about the people around us. "An unfriendly man pursues selfish ends" (Prov. 18:1). In addition, it can lead to a tremendous amount of grief as, "People who want to get rich fall into temptation and a trap and into many foolish and harmful desires that plunge men into ruin and destruction. For the love of money is a root of all kinds of evil. Some people, eager for money, have wandered from the faith and pierced themselves with many griefs" (1 Tim. 6:9–10). Certainly it seems innocent enough to hope that we could have it all, but when we pursue wealth, we inadvertently distance ourselves from others and from the Lord. We fail to recognize the temporary nature of earthly gain and become unwilling to wait for our inheritance in heaven.

Yet God commands us to not look to money or the accumulation of things, but to look to Him;

> Command those who are rich in this present world not to be arrogant nor to put their hope in wealth, which is so uncertain, but to put their hope in God, who richly provides us with everything for our enjoyment. Command them to do good, to be rich in good deeds, and to be generous and willing to share. In this way they will lay up treasure for themselves as a firm foundation for the coming age, so that they may take hold of the life that is truly life.
>
> —1 Timothy 6:17–19

What is the "life that is truly life?" It is your son's baseball game, your friends' wedding, your daughter's first cartwheel, lunch with your buddy, relationship with a loving God, and relationship with those whom He has placed in your life. It is also the hope of heaven. Many who put their hope in wealth miss those things in their pursuit of more.

We must resist the temptation to put our hope in wealth. Certainly wealth can make life more comfortable, but it should not be our hope. Our hope is in God and in the life to come, when we can enjoy all of the riches of God's

Kingdom. This life is only temporary, and we cannot take our accumulation of things with us into eternal life. Even King David noted, "Do not be overawed when a man grows rich, when the splendor of his house increases; for he will take nothing with him when he dies" (Ps. 49:16). Therefore, we need to take that into consideration when we decide where to invest our time, our energy, and our resources.

SHARE

If we are blessed with wealth, we are encouraged in Scripture to share our wealth with others. Randy Alcorn states in his book, *The Treasure Principle*, that the reason God blesses us is for a purpose and "not so we can indulge ourselves and spoil our children....It's so we can *give*—generously".

Recently I watched a TV special about the Fortune 500 list of wealthiest people in the world, and the discussion was about hoarding wealth and the egos of the wealthy. A new list was constructed to recognize the biggest givers and to encourage a shift. Some of the excessively wealthy changed their focus to be recognized on the biggest givers list. When interviewed a second time, they seemed happier and more satisfied to be helping others with their money rather than keeping it all for themselves.

DEPEND ON GOD

Putting our hope in earthly things is not just a struggle for the wealthy. Recently, I have come to believe that I cannot live without my cell phone. Accustomed to having it with me, I became convinced that I was dependant on it. Even the thought of not having it on me sent waves of anxiety through me. I considered the inconveniences and worried about emergencies. Then I lost my cell phone.

Since I tend to look for meaning in my circumstances, I considered and prayed about why I had lost it. One thing I became aware of was that I didn't miss it nearly as much as I had anticipated. As a matter of fact, it was a bit freeing not to have it with me. God reminded me that I needed to depend on Him not on my cell phone, and that what I think I must have I really don't need. What I do need is Him. "His divine power has given us everything we need for life and godliness through our knowledge of him who called us by his own glory and goodness" (2 Pet. 1:3). I can count on Him to provide for me and to protect me.

GOD PROVIDES

One reason the desire for wealth is so toxic is that it corrupts our minds and our actions. It can lead to taking advantage of others, tax evasion, felonious record changing, and in extreme cases, even murder. Just a few weeks ago a man was shot and killed in downtown Denver for his gold necklace. It happens both in upper class and in impoverished areas as well. The sad reality is that the value of the item or items becomes more important than the life of the person who possessed it. Scripture points out the faulty logic:

> Who is wise and understanding among you? Let him show it by his good life, by deeds done in the humility that comes from wisdom. But if you harbor bitter envy and *selfish ambition* in your hearts, do not boast about it or deny the truth. Such "wisdom" does not come down from heaven but is earthly, unspiritual, of the devil. For where you have envy and selfish ambition, there you find disorder and every evil practice.
>
> —James 3:13–16

The truth that we must cling to is that God loves us deeply and will provide all that we need and often all that we want. We errantly think that if we choose God over wealth, we will be denied what we want. But God says, "Delight yourself in the Lord and he will give you the desires of your heart" (Ps. 37:4). He also says, "But seek first his kingdom and his righteousness, and all these things will be given to you as well" (Matt. 6:33). When our hearts are in alignment with God and His will for our lives, He blesses us and takes care of our needs. We don't need to "wear ourselves out" seeking wealth when by seeking God and His kingdom we will be wealthy in spirit and will have all that we need on earth and will look forward to our heavenly "inheritance that can never perish, spoil, or fade—kept in heaven for you" (1 Pet. 1:4).

OBJECT PERMANENCE

Having an inheritance in heaven is very comforting, especially when money is so temporary and life is very expensive. However, since we cannot see heaven or what we are storing there, we lose sight of it and focus on what we can see instead. It is a bit similar to what psychologists who study infant development call "object permanence." A newborn infant will forget that something actually exists when it is hidden from him or her. Once he or she starts to develop object permanence he or she will look for the object after it has been hidden because he or she is able to understand that it still exists when it is out of sight. As Christians, we don't see our inheritance in heaven, but through the assurance of Scripture and the presence of the Holy Spirit, we believe that it does in fact exist even though we cannot see it.

Overflowing Blessings

When we have our hearts on heaven, we yearn to give to others. We feel blessed and full and taken care of, and it overflows into taking care of others in need. We don't feel competitive or afraid. In our security we are able to give to the poor as God commands us, knowing that we don't need to be afraid that we won't have what we need. "But when you give to the needy, do not let your left hand know what your right hand is doing, so that your giving may be in secret. Then your Father, who sees what is done in secret, will reward you" (Matt. 6:3–4). The Lord rewards us when we give privately, not openly for others to see. We must resist the temptation to show off and gain the attention of others.

Not letting our left hand know what our right hand does describes for us how we should even keep it secret from ourselves in the sense that we cannot allow pride to take root in our hearts. We give because we love and trust God, and because He commands us to. "Do nothing out of selfish ambition or vain conceit, but in humility consider others better than yourselves. Each of you should look not only to your own interests, but also to the interests of others" (Phil. 2:3–4). We do this also because we do not want to forfeit our reward from God. "So when you give to the needy, do not announce it with trumpets, as the hypocrites do in the synagogues and on the streets, to be honored by men. I tell you the truth; they have received their reward in full" (Matt. 6:2). Unless we are encouraging others to give, once we announce it to receive praise from others, we may have lost our chance to store our reward in heaven for us to enjoy for eternity.

RETAIN OUR REWARD

On the other hand, if we refrain from announcing it for recognition, we retain our reward from our Father in heaven. If we are overly focused on earthly gain, we will want that reward right away and may look for it to come monetarily and immediately. Some churches even emphasize earthly prosperity. This teaching is immature. Yes, sometimes God does reward us immediately, other times we wait. We may not even see the full extent of the reward until we are with our Father in heaven. We have faith that God will fulfill His promise to us.

We often struggle to shift our focus away from earthly gain and need to look to King David's example and cry out to God for help. "Direct me in the path of your commands, for there I find delight. Turn my heart toward your statutes and not toward selfish gain. Turn my eyes away from worthless things; preserve my life according to your word" (Ps. 119:35–37). David was humble enough to know that he needed God's help. David had access to great wealth, yet he cried out to God to help him maintain his focus on heavenly things, on the things that matter to God. Deep down David knew that selfish gain was worth nothing in the grand picture of God's will.

GIVING OUT

If our hearts are in this world and all it has to offer, we will be disinclined to give away a portion of our income to ministry or to the poor. Just the thought of it tugs at our hearts, and we start thinking about what we could use the extra money for—savings, the next upgrade, a newer car, and a few new outfits for the next season. Even for those of us who struggle to make ends meet, we think about food on the table, clothes for the kids, school supplies, the mortgage, and we fear we cannot afford to give. Yet, all of us who trust in God are thoroughly challenged to:

> Remember this: Whoever sows sparingly will also reap sparingly, and whoever sows generously will also reap generously. Each man should give what he has decided in his heart to give, not reluctantly or under compulsion, for God loves a cheerful giver. And God is able to make all grace abound to you, so that in all things at all times; *having all that you need*, you will abound in every good work. As it is written: "He has scattered abroad his gifts to the poor; his righteousness endures forever."
> —2 Corinthians 9:6–9, emphasis mine

Do we trust in God's promise that He will take care of us when we give to others? This is definitely an area that stretches our faith and challenges us to fall forward, trusting that God will catch us. The only sure way to experience God's provision financially is to surrender your finances to Him and trust that He "knows what you need before you ask" (Matt. 6:8). It is important to ask for God's provision in your life out of respect and relationship with Him. He requires that we ask even though He knows what we need. For example, I have needed a new pair of dark brown summer sandals since my old ones are worn out. Just the other day I found a pair in my size that I love for only $7.00! When we are in His will He loves to bless us abundantly.

I hear people ask, "Why do I have to ask if He already knows what I need?" The answer is that He yearns for relationship with you. God is not a giant pinball machine in the sky that delivers what you need when you put a coin in the slot. He is a loving, kind, and compassionate God who calls you "friend," and that means He desires relationship with you through prayer. Talk to Him about what you need and even about what you want.

PRACTICAL GIVING

I have been a part of activities where the church gave to the community. We cleaned single moms' homes, gave food to the homeless, gave Christmas gifts to children, and served one another. At Smoky Hill Vineyard we have a ministry called *The Net Food Pantry* that gives out food and clothing to the poor in our neighborhood on a regular basis. Having been on a tight budget before, I am at least slightly in touch with the struggle of low-income families to make ends meet, especially when there are children involved. We must make it a part of our active faith to give to others. We are assured that "although they cannot repay you, you will be repaid at the resurrection of the righteous" (Luke 14:14).

We receive consistent encouragement to "see that you also excel in this grace of giving" (2 Cor. 8:7). Once you catch on to the blessing that giving brings to your life, you will never go back to a life of hoarding. The things that I give away are the things that I have in abundance. One thing our house never lacks is clothing for our kids. I believe that part of the reason for this abundance is that we give their clothes away rather than selling them on Ebay or at a garage sale. The moment we give clothes away, more come in. When we share with others, God makes sure we are abundantly provided for. Ecclesiastes says, "Cast your bread upon the waters, for after many days you will find it again" (Ecc.11:1).

POINTS TO CONSIDER: SELFISHNESS VS. GIVING

- Modern culture promotes selfishness and having more, bigger, and better.
- We trust that God will provide for us and give us an inheritance in heaven.

- God blesses us when we are in His will and when we give to others.

EXPLORATION QUESTIONS

1. Am I selfish sometimes? In what areas?
2. Do I seek wealth or status over relationship with God? In what ways?
3. Do I give a portion of my income to ministry or to the poor? If not, what keeps me from giving?
4. How have I experienced God's provision and blessing in my life?

FOCUS VERSE

Now he who supplies seed to the sower and bread for food will also supply and increase your store of seed and will enlarge the harvest of your righteousness. You will be made rich in every way so that you can be generous on every occasion, and through us your generosity will result in thanksgiving to God.

—2 Corinthians 9:10–11

FOCUS PRAYER

Lord, I am sorry that I seek after things and for being selfish. Help me to trust that You will provide for all of my needs. I know that if I give to Your kingdom purposes, You will make sure I am taken care of abundantly. Help me surrender my finances to You and give others what You call me to give. In Jesus' name, amen.

CHAPTER 12

THE WEED OF HASTE
VS.
THE FRUIT OF PATIENCE

Haste—a state in which somebody is moving or doing
something with great or excessive speed because of a real
or perceived lack of time.
—Encarta Dictionary

MY OWN STRUGGLE WITH HASTE

ON MY WAY to my cousin's wedding, I realized I had
seriously miscalculated how long it would take to get
there by about an hour. Once I discovered my error, I was
unable to accept the fact that I would be late (perfectionism),
so I began to speed. Hurriedly, I careened in and out of
traffic at over 90 miles per hour. God's angels must have
been looking out for me (and everyone around me) because
I was driving fast and recklessly, determined to get there
on time.

Once I arrived, I parked the car, fled into the building,
and said a quick hello to the bride and groom standing
at the doorway as I scurried past them and down to my
seat in the front. Plowing down the aisle, I confused the

congregation—some who started to stand and then sat back down, bewildered—as it was the moment the bride and groom were to make their grand entrance. The bridesmaids were already down front, and the formal Catholic service had begun, but I was so focused on my relief that I had made it on time that I hadn't realized what I had done.

Fortunately, the couple has been good humored about my untimely appearance down the aisle on their wedding day. I hear them chuckle and say, "Wait, here comes Gretchen," when they watch the wedding video. Truthfully, I had been in such a frenetic hurry that day it didn't occur to me until months later what had happened. Once I realized, I thought *Oh no! What did I do?!*

RACE AGAINST THE CLOCK

This rushed pace is reflected in other areas of my life as well. Everywhere I used to go, I would race against the clock. I was so frequently in a hurry that even if I didn't need to rush, I would compulsively pick up the pace. It was hard for me to enjoy the moment wherever I was because I would constantly check the clock for the time. I would speed in traffic, cut off people in conversation, and focus on the next thing instead of enjoying where I was at the time. One thing that drove my pace was the need to be productive and to be a part of something important. I filled my schedule with too many things, so indeed I was in a hurry to get from one thing to the next and to complete tasks in time for the next task. Being busy helped me to feel important, a part of something...needed.

One event that made me realize I needed to change my frenetic pace was when I was on the way to a prayer meeting for church and got a speeding ticket. Granted, it was a "speed trap" since the speed limit went from 45 to 25 without much warning. Still I failed to slow down, because I was going to be late. Upon arrival, I realized that everyone was relaxed and that I hadn't really missed much anyway. It occurred to me that I hadn't needed to be in such a rush. Later, when receiving prayer, someone noted that he felt the Holy Spirit had impressed on him that God wanted me to "slow down."

I would like to say that my "aha" moment led to immediate freedom from what plagued me, but I must be honest that the process took years to change. Even now after I have succeeded in changing this habit, I can revert back to it during times of external stress or even self-imposed pressure. In paying attention to myself, I figured out that there were several reasons behind my haste and busyness, such as pleasing others, over-responsibility, fear of disapproval. I could even think of some events in my life that contributed to it. However, I also realized that the primary task at hand involved changing habits and that took a lot of practice.

BREAKDOWN

One thing I learned is that God was not putting this pressure on me. In fact, He was trying to take it off. It was I who continued to pick up the burden and embrace the weight of becoming busy taking care of everyone but myself. I was rushing from one thing to the next, always pre-occupied with what needed to be done. Many of you can relate to this frenetic pace of doing too many things and trying to make sure everyone is happy.

For me, the big test came during a time when I was doing way too much—leading a ministry at my church, working full time as an addictions counselor, helping others with their ministries, and living under a tremendous amount of stress in my personal relationships. When I was usually able to pull through anything, I think God allowed me to get beyond my own capacity to manage so that I could learn this lesson once and for all. Once I realized I was beyond my capacity to manage, I tried to attain others approval to step down from ministry. When I didn't get that, but knew I could no longer please others at my own expense, I chose to step down from leading ministry without anyone saying it was okay except God.

During communion I heard from the Holy Spirit that it was okay with Him that I step down and that He loved me deeply apart from what I did. I asked, "Really?" because I didn't quite believe it. I was so nervous that I was shaking when I handed in my resignation letter saying I would be stepping down a few months shy of my one-year commitment. This went against everything I was comfortable with—pleasing others, being busy, being needed. I had no choice because I knew I was close to a breakdown and barely hanging on.

Indeed, a few weeks later I did break down. My body collapsed in tremendous fatigue and exhaustion. I could barely function as I had once functioned. I also had to take a medical leave from work because the cumulative stress led to such a high degree of burnout I was unable to function at work. Shut down, all I could do was sleep and rest at home... even that seemed like too much. I truly had come to the end of myself, and it would take years to recover fully.

God Gives Rest

Coming to the end of myself has been the most valuable lesson I have ever had in my life, partly because I finally get it now. I *do not* want to have to go through that lesson again. That realization prevents me from going back to my old ways.

However, the primary reason I don't want to go back to my old ways is that I have learned the freedom that comes when I am in God's will, when I am seeking to please God and not the people around me. I learned that other people's happiness is not my responsibility. My responsibility is to follow God's leading and rely on His grace or favor in my life. It is amazing to me how much more bearable it is to be a part of God's plan and aligned with His will. I experienced the rest that He promises when we come to Him. "Come to me, all you who are weary and burdened, and I will give you rest. Take my yoke upon you and learn from me, for I am gentle and humble in heart, and you will find rest for your souls. For my yoke is easy and my burden is light" (Matt. 11:28–30).

I learned that God's timing is different than the world's timing, and that I didn't need to be in such a tremendous hurry. "But do not forget this one thing, dear friends: With the Lord a day is like a thousand years, and a thousand years are like a day. The Lord is not slow in keeping his promise, as some understand slowness. He is patient with you, not wanting anyone to perish, but everyone to come to repentance" (2 Pet. 3:8–9). I am grateful that He was patient enough with me to unwearyingly wait until I figured it out and could genuinely repent of my fast-paced, hurried lifestyle and desperate need to please others, many who seemed un-please-able.

RELIEF AND HOPE

Once I got it, and experienced God's grace and presence and leading in my life as I slowed down, I began to experience relief and hope. It was such a relief to know that God was pleased with me. I didn't need to run around so fast doing things I thought were important to please Him. He was already pleased with me. He already loved me. I could collapse into His arms and stop everything I was doing and just be loved by Him as I recovered from my own haste. What a marvelous blessing it was for me to experience that love and acceptance when my fast pace all along had been driven by a fear of rejection and disapproval. I learned that the only approval I needed was from God and God alone. My security now resides fully in Him. Having experienced His patience with me, I could learn to be patient with myself, with others, and with life. Jesus teaches a way of life, and patience is a key component of it. "You, however, know all about my teaching, my way of life, my purpose, faith, patience, love, endurance" (2 Tim. 3:10). For us to be followers of Jesus, we must learn patience.

Our haste can reveal itself at many different times, such as when someone is driving too slowly in front of us. We are quick to become irritated with how others are driving, when really we waited too long to leave and are running late. We become narcissistic, meaning we are self-centered. We think everyone should be aware that we are in a hurry and should get out of our way. We think others should automatically be aware of our needs and rush to cater to them. Getting easily irritated hinders us from an ability to refocus and see what is going on in the world around us. If we are in a rush, we expect others to be in a rush too, and the world becomes a frustrating place.

LEARNING PATIENCE

I was enjoying a sunny walk on the day I had initially asked God to teach me patience. Since I was still young, I naively thought I would be zapped with patience. I thought I could suddenly be magnificently patient with everyone around me, as if struck with sudden super-powers. I soon realized my ability to be patient would only come through a series of tests that would try my patience. I suddenly ended up in the longest line in the grocery store—every time. Or if I attempted to approach a shorter line, the tape in the cash register would jam, and I would have to calm my need to rush through that line. I have lost count of the times the tape jammed as I approached the cashier. Gradually, I learned to take a few deep breaths and accept the fact that I was going to need to wait rather than huff and puff and become angry. Now, if that happens, I smile and tell about how I asked God to teach me patience. Usually I get a strange look, but I figure it is a chance to share.

Patience often does not come automatically, because our earthly flesh wants what it wants and wants it now. We are not so different from the typical four-year-old. My four-year-old son really does not have a concept of time. When I ask him to wait, he gets restless and asks for what he wants repeatedly. If I continue to ask him to wait, he takes things into his own hands. For example, the other day he wanted to paint. I asked him to wait until I finished an email to get his paints out. He pestered me until he disappeared. Relieved, I finished my email in peace, only to find that he had gone downstairs and pulled out the paints and accidentally squirted yellow paint all over the beige chair. How often in our strong sense of urgency do we take things into our own hands, without waiting for God, and make a mess? More often than we would like to admit!

FINANCIAL IMPLICATIONS

The proverbs describe patience as "great understanding" and "wisdom" and the lack of it as "quick-tempered" and "folly" (Prov. 14:29 and Prov. 19:11). Recently, I saw on the news some victims of a financial scam. Many of them had lost life savings and ruined their credit rating due to a hasty decision. If we are hasty in important financial decisions, it can lead to ruin. Yet, if we take time to consider our decisions and do our research, we can do well. "The plans of the diligent lead to profit as surely as haste leads to poverty" (Prov. 21:5).

I have learned never to make a decision under pressure. If someone is pressuring me to decide without giving me time to think, I take that as a cue to say "no, thank you" and move on. Pressured sales are all about not wanting you to think since you will realize it is not a good idea once you consider the facts. Financial decisions should always be made with diligence. When my husband and I were looking for a home, we put money down on a condo because we felt afraid someone else would get it. Even the sales women urged us saying, "If you don't put money down now, you could lose it." Once we thought about it and discussed it, we realized we didn't want the condo. Fortunately, we got our money back from our "hold," and we drove past it months later and saw that it was still available. We are both very glad that we didn't buy it, because God had a better home for us with a backyard for the kids to play in.

GOD'S PROTECTION WHEN WE WAIT

When we wait on God, we are sheltered in His care. My son would not have made a mess of the yellow paint that was difficult to clean up if he had waited for me to help him. When we wait for God's timing, we have the Lord's assistance. I have experienced that when I do things on my own timing and my own strength, things don't usually go as well as planned, and I end up exhausted. When we are synchronized with the Lord's leading, we are much more able to accomplish our goals and even go beyond them. God promises that, "You will not leave in haste or go in flight; for the LORD will go before you, the God of Israel will be your rear guard. See, my servant will act wisely; he will be raised and lifted up and highly exalted" (Isa. 52:12–13). When we take the time to consider our steps and pray and seek God, we make wiser choices and the Lord is with us.

I used to fear that I would mess up God's plans for me if I hesitated or made the wrong decision. I felt a tremendous amount of fear around my decisions. This is a failure to understand God's sovereignty and ability to carry us through. When we seek Him in our decisions, and learn to discern His leading, He cares for us, and we won't miss out on His plans even if we make some mistakes. Mistakes are a wonderful opportunity to learn, and God's grace covers us. When God knows our hearts desire is to follow Him, His Holy Spirit reveals to us what we need to learn and enables us to grow.

ALWAYS A CHALLENGE

The truth is that I wish I were more patient than I actually am. My children often try my patience. Much to my dismay, I sometimes lose patience when I need it the most. I can be quite patient when all I have to think about is my kids. However, when I have other things and timelines pressing on me, I tend to become impatient and frustrated with how long it takes them to do just about anything. If you want to learn patience, just spend some extended time with children. I don't mean just play with them, but be in charge of them for a while, and they will push you past your limits with a tenacity that will baffle you. Just the effort toward patience with children can lead to exhaustion.

GOD IS PATIENT WITH US

Understanding children gives us a bird's-eye view of how patient God is with us. Over and over again we try

His patience with rebellion, with resistance, and by straying from His will, just as children test the rules and limits to see if you care enough to correct them. Similarly, when it is time to get my daughter into her pajamas, she runs away from me as fast as she can. She hides, and when I catch her she sometimes, in true toddler form, kicks and wiggles away from me. I know she needs the warmth of her pajamas, but she just wants to do what she wants to do. We fail to recognize that when God extends His love to us we often do the same. We run the other direction, choosing sin and disobedience rather than accepting his help and provision.

The Apostle Paul described it this way: "But for that very reason I was shown mercy so that in me, the worst of sinners, Christ Jesus might display his unlimited patience as an example for those who would believe on Him and receive eternal life" (1 Tim. 1:16). The Lord is amazingly patient with us. And He asks us to be the same. "Be completely humble and gentle; be patient, bearing with one another in love" (Eph. 4:2). There is fruit in patience and in waiting on the Lord's leading. Rather then running ahead of Him, stay in His will and His presence, and He will give you rest. He will also lead you in His plans for you—plans that will surpass your own.

POINTS TO CONSIDER: HASTE VS. PATIENCE

- Haste prevents us from enjoying the present and keeps us preoccupied with what's next.
- Patience keeps us in alignment with God's timing.
- When we understand God's patience with us, we can also be more patient with others.

EXPLORATION QUESTIONS

1. What am I in a hurry about?
2. How is Jesus patient with me?
3. How can I slow down and learn patience?
4. What is the benefit of learning patience?

FOCUS VERSE

Obey the king's command, I say, because you took an oath before God. Do not be in a hurry to leave the king's presence. Do not stand up for a bad cause, for he will do whatever he pleases. Since a king's word is supreme, who can say to him, "What are you doing?"

—Ecclesiastes 8:2–4

FOCUS PRAYER

Lord, I am sorry for being in such a hurry. Help me to slow down and learn Your patience. Thank You for being patient with me when I have needed Your patience. Help me to stay in Your will and not be in a rush to accomplish too many things. In Jesus' name, amen.

CHAPTER 13

THE WEED OF PRIDE VS. THE FRUIT OF RELATIONSHIP

CALLED TO RELATIONSHIP

WE ARE CALLED to be in relationship with God and not just to follow a bunch of rules. Merely following rules is tedious and empty without relationship. It is important that we understand our faith in the context of a relationship that is active and current. What do we do when we are with our friends? We talk, we laugh, we cry, we listen, and we care deeply about each other. We enjoy their company and spend time together.

If we want to maintain our friendships, we must make an effort to stay in touch. We talk on the phone, email, or we schedule time together. We think not only of ourselves, but also of our friends. We reciprocate, invest time, and we are considerate of our friends. We miss them when they are away, and we make a point to make time for them. Our first and primary calling as believers is to a relationship with God.

HOLY SPIRIT COUNSELOR

Without relationship with God, the personal growth we do comes out of a self-centered focus. Although it can be beneficial, when personal growth centers around "self" it lacks the depth of healing that a relationship with God can offer. It comes out of our own effort and our own strength, which is quite limited. I can say that the deep-rooted changes and inner growth that I have encountered have been fully sourced by the presence of the Holy Spirit in my life. Jesus said that when His physical body returned to heaven with the Father, He would send the Holy Spirit to us. The Holy Spirit is the presence of the Lord in our hearts. He is our Counselor, who guides us and enables us to grow in faith and understanding. "But the Counselor, the Holy Spirit, whom the Father will send in my name, will teach you all things and will remind you of everything I have said to you" (John 14:26). He comes to us in the context of love to be present with us in our daily lives. When we love the Lord, the Holy Spirit dwells within us.

> If you love me, you will obey what I command. And I will ask the Father, and he will give you another Counselor to be with you forever—the Spirit of truth. The world cannot accept him, because it neither sees him nor knows him. But you know him, for he lives with you and will be in you. I will not leave you as orphans; I will come to you. Before long, the world will not see me anymore, but you will see me. Because I live, you also will live. On that day you will realize that I am in my Father, and you are in me, and I am in you. Whoever has my commands and obeys them, he is the one who loves me. He who loves me will be loved by my Father, and I too will love him and show myself to him.
>
> —John 14:15–21

We must understand that loving the Lord is a choice. We do not love the Lord out of guilt or obligation or coercion. He does not force us to love Him. "We love because he first loved us" (1 John 4:19). I know that I have been transformed by God's love into a new person. His love has changed me, yet I would not have experienced that change unless I had decided to return His love. I chose to love God in return.

God's Love for Others

Recently I was on an airplane, sitting next to a young girl who was very bright and engaging. I could tell from our conversation that she didn't know the Lord. As we spoke, I suddenly felt a tremendous amount of love for her. I realized that it was the Holy Spirit showing me in my spirit how much He loves her. I wished I had said more to her about God's love, but I was distracted by my restless one-year-old daughter, who was not traveling well. Instead, I prayed for her that someday she will know and experience the transforming power of God's love in her heart rather than the materials things she talked about—purses, shoes, and fashion.

When we witness to people about faith in God, the primary focus should be on the Lord's love for them, because we are not trying to convert people to a religion that is created by man, but to a relationship with Jesus, who guides us with His love and the presence of the Holy Spirit. Relationship and love are the primary focus, because they are our first calling and are what true faith is about.

We not only want to enjoy our relationship with the Lord, but also to grow in faith. Jesus shows us the weeds in our garden and lovingly helps us remove them. It is important that we engage in this process within the context of relationship with Him and not as an effort to follow rules.

The fruit of this is that others see our love for the Lord and may begin to desire it for themselves.

LOVE IS THE CENTER POINT

Jesus asks us to hold love as a center point of our relationship with Him. "As the Father has loved me, so have I loved you. Now remain in my love" (John 15:9). We must stay in His love. Notice that the use of the word "remain" indicates an ongoing choice. We can easily stray away from love and relationship. I have friends I didn't intend to lose contact with, but life became busy or distance came between us, and I did. I wish I was more able to stay in contact with the people I have encountered in friendship, but it is not physically possible for me to do that.

I have also experienced the loss of close friends in my life. Being an only child, I tended to long for close friendships. I have yearned for close relationship so much that I have depended too much on them. When I lost the friends that I had devoted so much of my time and energy to, I felt devastated and disoriented.

Recovering from those losses, I learned that the only true and consistent friend is Jesus. He always wants to be close to me. I recognized that when I depended too strongly on people, I began to idolize the friendship, and I attempted to attain from that friendship what only God could give me consistently and thoroughly enough to satisfy my soul in its deepest depths. Jesus says that He relates to us as friends when He explains, "I no longer call you servants, because a servant does not know his master's business. Instead, I have called you friends, for everything that I learned from my Father I have made known to you" (John 15:15). As we lean into the Lord in our trials, our daily life, and in our joys, He teaches us His ways and enables us to walk in them by the power and presence of the Holy Spirit.

He chose us not only to be in relationship with us, but also to be fruitful in our lives. "You did not choose me, but I chose you and appointed you to go and bear fruit—fruit that will last. Then the Father will give you whatever you ask in my name. This is my command: Love each other" (John 15:16–17). When He comes and does the weeding in our lives, we may protest at the discomfort it causes, but He has a larger picture in mind for us. His vision for us goes beyond just existing. It involves a fruitful and productive life. He is not just weeding our garden to make us fruitful in this temporary life, but also for eternity.

LEARNING TO RECOGNIZE HIS VOICE

God is speaking to us all the time. Most of us aren't listening. We are too busy going about our business, and hearing His voice is often outside of our perception of what is possible in our lives. We might think it is "crazy" to hear God's voice, or we might fear that He will ask us to do something we don't want to do. We may never have understood the Scripture verses that say His followers know His voice. "I am the good shepherd; I know my sheep and my sheep know me—just as the Father knows me and I know the Father—and I lay down my life for the sheep" (John 10:14–16), and "my sheep listen to my voice; I know them, and they follow me" (John 10:27).

Following Jesus involves knowing His voice and learning to tune in to His presence in our hearts. If we are not expecting Him to speak to us, we won't bother listening. If we are expectant and hopeful that He can and will speak to us, then we will begin to perceive His voice in our spirits.

I know that many are concerned and ask, "How do you know that it is the Holy Spirit speaking to you and not your own spirit or an evil spirit?" I think that question is a great one and one that should be explored. First of all, the Holy Spirit will never contradict Scripture. Therefore, it is really important if you want to hear God's voice to be familiar with His Word and to be reading Scripture regularly. Second, the Holy Spirit will not make you feel afraid or fearful. He may convict you or give a warning, but it will feel clean and will be supported by His love and presence. This assures that He will help you to change and walk in His will. His voice is loving and gentle.

Third, it is important to pray about it and ask for discernment. Also, don't be afraid to make mistakes. This doesn't mean impulsively follow every voice in your head, but be willing to take risks as you try to follow God's leading. In prayer ask God to teach you. That is how you will learn. I have heard it said before that it is impossible to drive a parked car. The Holy Spirit will only be able to guide you if you are willing to put the gears of your life in drive and allow Him to do the steering. You will not regret it.

WILLING TO RESPOND

If we desire to hear His voice, we must be willing to respond. Some of us are not ready to fully surrender our lives to Him. We dip our toes into church and faith, as we do to test the temperature before we go swimming. But many of us don't go much farther than that. Others may go in ankle- or knee-deep, but they hesitate to go further.

A friend of mine shared a story about her niece that reflects this hesitancy we all feel at first. Her niece had been learning about Jesus, and her mom was talking with her about Him. Her mom gently explained that we need to invite

Jesus into our hearts. She asked her daughter if she would like to do that. Her daughter's answer was very honest and direct, "No, because I think He would get in my way." I love that response, because it is so honest and reveals our inner human nature that is inclined to resist God. Deep down we all want to do it our own way.

We all have pride in our hearts, and we want to be right and know what we are doing on our own. I have done things both ways—on my own terms and on God's terms—and I can attest that God's terms have always had better results in my life. Because I know that, I choose God's way and seek relationship with Him and invite Him into every major decision in my life. I often ask for His opinion on small things too, because we are encouraged to "pray continually" (1 Thess. 5:17). When we pray continually, we talk to God all the time about whatever is on our minds. We can do this in the car, in the grocery aisle, doing dishes, and wherever we are. When we are praying continually and inviting God into our daily activities, we are more likely to be in alignment with His will and to hear His voice.

HOLY SPIRIT DEPOSIT

God gives us His spirit to dwell within us when we have faith in Him. He instructs us to guard that deposit He gives to us. "What you heard from me, keep as the pattern of sound teaching, with faith and love in Christ Jesus. Guard the good deposit that was entrusted to you—guard it with the help of the Holy Spirit who lives in us" (2 Tim. 1:13–14).

His Holy Spirit indwelling our hearts is an assurance of our inheritance in heaven (2 Cor. 1:21–22). He is "guaranteeing what is to come" (2 Cor. 1:22). I don't know about you, but that gives me tremendous hope! I look forward to the future and have less fear of the present struggles because I know for certain that this life is temporary, and therefore, the struggles I face are temporary. Experiencing His presence with me as I go through life's challenges makes them more bearable.

Part of guarding the Holy Spirit in our hearts is to pull out the weeds that hinder our spiritual growth. The Holy Spirit will guide and instruct us, but we must be teachable, humble, and willing to embark on that journey. If we are not humble, we are warned that "God opposes the proud, but gives grace to the humble" (James 4:6). It involves humility to allow the weeds to be exposed and pulled from our lives. The fruit is a stronger and closer relationship with the Lord.

Some Christian circles teach a type of religion that involves wealth and a comfortable life, yet that is not what Jesus taught. We have wealth in our souls and wealth in our future inheritance, but we are told that "in this world you will have trouble. But take heart! I have overcome the world" (John 16:33). We have a faith that has already overcome the struggles of this life. It is important to understand that we aren't spared from struggles, but we are given hope that we can look forward to a future that is free from agony and heartache. Doesn't that give you great hope?!

RELATIONSHIP WITH OTHERS

Not only are we called to be in relationship with our heavenly Father, whom we have full access to because of Jesus' sacrifice and through the indwelling of the Holy Spirit, but also we are called to be in relationship with each other. We do this so that we can support each other as we are instructed. "Let us consider how we may spur one another on toward love and good deeds. Let us not give up meeting together, as some are in the habit of doing, but let us encourage one another—and all the more as you see the

Day approaching" (Heb. 10:24–25). We must not get in the habit of being on our own. This is not a solo faith, this is a life in which we need others to support us, encourage us, and help us practically.

In my experience in Christian community, I have been prayed for more times than I can count, I have been listened to, given meals when I had a baby, helped to move by others carrying boxes and cleaning. These things were all a tremendous support for me during times that I needed it. Relationships add richness and comfort to our lives.

OUR GREATEST COMFORT

The greatest comfort is that Jesus was a Friend of "sinners" (Luke 7:34). That means I can be His friend no matter what I have done in the past. He says that if we "come near to God (and) he will come near to you (us)" (James 4:8). If you ask Him to, He will be the closest friend you will ever have. However, if you don't invite Him, He won't come near. He doesn't impose or force relationship on you. He waits to be sought out, and gives a promise that He will respond by becoming your trusted friend.

Additionally, we are to love each other as He has loved us (John 15:12), and love our neighbor as we love ourselves (Luke 10:27). Relationship with Jesus is the center point for our faith. We live under the new covenant in which "a better hope is introduced, by which we draw near to God" (Hebrews 7:18). Seek a closer, more intimate relationship with God. Don't just dip your toes in, go deeper. He will not disappoint you.

POINTS TO CONSIDER: PRIDE VS. RELATIONSHIP

- God desires for you to be in a loving relationship with Him.

- Love is the center point of relationship with God.
- Pride prevents us from experiencing deeper relationship with God.

EXPLORATION QUESTIONS

1. How important is relationship to me in my spiritual walk?
2. In what ways does my pride hinder my relationship with God?
3. What can I be doing to invest in my relationship with Jesus?
4. How can I become or stay a part of community?

FOCUS VERSE

"This is the covenant I will make with the house of Israel after that time," declares the Lord. "I will put my laws in their minds and write them on their hearts. I will be their God, and they will be my people. No longer will a man teach his neighbor, or a man his brother, saying, 'Know the Lord,' because they will all know me, from the least of them to the greatest. For I will forgive their wickedness and will remember their sins no more."

—Hebrews 8:10–12

PRAYER

Lord, thank You that you are not a distant God, but a God who loves to be in relationship with us. Forgive me for not taking the time to invest in my relationship with You by spending time in Your presence. Teach me to understand what it means to be Your friend and to hear Your voice. I love You, Lord, and I desire to be closer to You. Thanks for loving me, even when I am not faithful to You. In Jesus' name, amen.

CHAPTER 14

WHEN YOUR GARDEN GROWS— A HARVEST OF FRUITFULNESS

The righteous will flourish like a palm tree; they will grow like a cedar of Lebanon; planted in the house of the LORD, they will flourish in the courts of our God. They will still bear fruit in old age, they will stay fresh and green.

—Psalm 92:12–14

THE FRUIT OF JOY

IN ADDITION TO fruitfulness in the afore-mentioned areas: trust, peace, patience, confidence, contentment, compassion, repentance, forgiveness, gratitude, authenticity, giving, patience, and relationship, we also experience the fruit of joy in our lives. When we allow weeds to be pulled from our lives, and we surrender to the tilling of the soil, we prepare ourselves for a harvest of joy. We bear fruit. This is a testimony that God has truly done a healing work in us. "Yet He has shown us kindness by giving you rain from heaven and crops in their seasons; He provides you with plenty of food and fills your heart with joy" (Acts 14:17). He continues

189

to supply our needs and waters us with His Spirit so that we are fruitful in our daily lives and filled with joy.

When you are given instructions and encouraged to follow Jesus wholeheartedly, it is "so that (His) my joy may be in you and that your joy may be complete" (John 15:11). We are given not just partial joy, but complete joy. A complete joy is one that overrides circumstances and hardship. It is one given by the Holy Spirit (Romans 14:17) to encourage and strengthen us and give us the hope of heaven. "Now is your time of grief, but I will see you again and you will rejoice, and *no one will take away your joy*. In that day you will no longer ask me anything." And it gives us the hope of God's current provision: "I tell you the truth, my Father will give you whatever you ask in my name. Until now you have not asked for anything in my name. Ask and you will receive, and your *joy will be complete*" (John 16:22–24, emphasis mine).

HE ANOINTS US

When we pursue the tilling and plowing of the soil of our souls and grow in our faith, God blesses and anoints us. "You have loved righteousness and hated wickedness; therefore God, your God, has set you above your companions by anointing you with the oil of joy" (Heb. 1:9). It doesn't matter what we have done in the past, when we desire God's presence and seek Him, the result is joy, and we will begin to bear fruit in our lives as an outpouring of that joy. He anoints us, and through His favor we are blessed.

God promises that even in the midst of hardship and persecution…"the disciples were filled with joy and with the Holy Spirit" (Acts 13:52). Scriptures assure us that we will experience hardship as we seek to follow Jesus and do God's will in our lives. I know that I have experienced struggles that brought me to despair and to question. Yet the only place I wanted to be was in God's will, because I have always known that He can be trusted to carry me through and to lead me to "green pastures" (Ps. 23:2). As I have leaned into the Lord during those times of struggle, rather than give up hope, I have experienced breakthroughs and changes that I am certain came only through God's grace and healing. I have experienced joy even when I was facing hardship. The joy God gives goes far beyond any amount of "happiness" that the world tries to offer.

One of my favorite passages creates a picture for us that is not free of pain, but it promises that what we suffer leads to great hope that "those who sow in tears will reap with songs of joy. He who goes out weeping, carrying seed to sow, will return with songs of joy, carrying sheaves with him" (Ps. 126:5–6). Because I have experienced many tears in my life, this verse comforts me. It comforts me that the lessons I have learned through hardship and the choices I have made that have led to goodbyes and an unknown future, will be worthwhile in the long run and will produce joy.

MEASURED BY OUR HEARTS

The world measures fruitfulness by the accumulation of wealth, but that is not God's way. God does not measure the harvest that way, He looks at the heart. "But the wisdom that comes from heaven is first of all pure; then peace-loving, considerate, submissive, full of mercy and good fruit, impartial, and sincere. Peacemakers who sow in peace raise a harvest of righteousness" (James 3:17–18). God measures fruitfulness by the sincerity of our hearts and character traits that God values, including loving His mercy and peace. Sometimes we think of fruitfulness in more tangible terms, such as a church plant or starting a new ministry. But

Scripture repeatedly states that God is often first interested in our character development.

THE LORD SUPPLIES WHAT WE NEED

When our hearts are in relationship with Him, then He "supplies seed to the sower and bread for food," and it is God who will "supply and increase your store of seed and will enlarge the harvest of your righteousness" (2 Cor. 9:10). We clearly cannot do this on our own. He supplies what we need and the direction for our lives as we stay connected with Him. Once we have allowed Him to weed our garden, we can present fertile soil for the seed to be planted in and to grow unhindered by the things that choke out our fruitfulness.

We can trust His plans for us and know that they are good. "'For I know the plans I have for you,' declares the LORD, 'plans to prosper you and not to harm you, plans to give you hope and a future. Then you will call upon me and come and pray to me, and I will listen to you'" (Jer. 29:11–12). If we align ourselves with His will, He promises that we will be provided for and that His plans for us are good.

ETERNAL VALUE

The harvest that we experience is twofold: internally we are changed and experience a *harvest of righteousness*, and externally we bear fruit in our interactions with others as we serve each other and share our hope with others. The fruit we bear in our lives brings us to a new place in our ability to walk in freedom and uprightness. In doing so, we are also able to externally impact the world around us in a way that has eternal value.

I have often said that I want to be a part of things that have eternal value. I admit I have often been uncertain of what exactly that meant practically speaking, but my heart desired it and still does. So what does this mean? If we want to be invested in things that have eternal rather than temporal value, we must understand that we are also a part of the seed sowing process in the choices we make. If we sow "to please the Spirit, from the Spirit (we) will reap eternal life." On the contrary, if we sow to indulge "the sinful nature, from that nature (we) will reap destruction" (Gal. 6:8). Destruction doesn't necessarily mean that something horrible will happen, it can mean that it won't last. If we spend most of our time and finances focusing on material things, such as manicures or fashion or electronics, we are investing in things that will in the end be destroyed. They won't last. They don't have staying power.

The things that do have staying power and will not be destroyed at the end of time are the things that have eternal value. Those are the things that we will benefit from investing in long term. We may never see the full result of our efforts in this lifetime, but we trust that God's Scripture is true and that we can in fact store up treasure in heaven (Matt. 6:20).

Living out God's plans for our lives involves surrendering our own plans. If we hold too tightly to a worldly, and therefore limited, vision for our lives, we will miss out on the harvest that God promises we can have. God's plans for us are built into who we are and what we are naturally inclined towards. "For we are God's workmanship, created in Christ Jesus to do good works, which God prepared in advance for us to do" (Eph. 2:10). He has already prepared the way. The question is whether or not we discover it, pursue it, and choose it rather than limit ourselves to what the world has to offer.

Harvest Time

There comes a time in our lives when God has tilled the soil and yanked out the weeds and we are ready to go out and do His work. His work might mean many different things. Many of us are afraid to seek God's will because we fear we might have to give up our job and move to a remote jungle and minister to indigenous people in undeveloped areas. I suppose that might be a possibility, but it is more likely that He is calling you to pursue Him in your daily life and daily interactions with others and to be *Christ-like* in the way you interact with the people God loves. This means that you carry the traits He values—"love, joy, peace, patience, kindness, goodness, faithfulness, gentleness, and self-control" (Gal. 5: 22) in your interactions with others at the office, during your lunch break, and with family and friends. Then be in a stance of readiness "to give an answer to everyone who asks you to give the reason for the hope that you have" (1 Pet. 3:15).

In addition, we need to pursue His will in our lives and to be aware that there is a great need for us to be available to God for His purposes. Jesus told His disciples, "The harvest is plentiful, but the workers are few. Ask the Lord of the harvest, therefore, to send out workers into his harvest field" (Luke 10:2). Pray for His kingdom purposes to be accomplished and seek His will for your life. It may mean we take a different path than the one we are currently on, but chances are it will be far more satisfying, and it will have eternal value.

SUPPORT MISSIONARIES

If we are not going ourselves, we must be praying for those who are out on the mission fields doing His "frontline" work. We can also support missionaries financially if we have the means to go above our tithe. This is how we store up treasure in heaven rather than on earth. If we put money in the bank or toward a new pair of shoes, then it stops there, but if we give it to His work around the world, it has eternal value and will go toward your eternal inheritance. Of course this does not mean that you are careless with your finances, but that you consider carefully a ministry or cause that you could give to that will benefit God's kingdom purposes.

PRACTICAL MINISTRY

There are many ways to become involved at different levels. Possibly your church needs a greeter or someone to set up and take down, or maybe you can serve on the prayer team or at your kid's school. You do not have to be a leader to be a part of what God is doing. Possibly all you have time to do is to intercede for others while you are driving your car or unloading the dishwasher. Intercession is a wonderful ministry that extends God's grace to people. You can even pray for people around the world. It is important to always be praying and asking God to lead you and help you to be willing to follow. There have been many times when I have been involved in very mundane tasks, but that is where God placed me at the time. Sometimes during those mundane, unnoticed tasks I learned some of the most important character lessons. Sometimes God is preparing us for what He wants us to do. We shouldn't hurry the process, but be willing to follow God's leading in our lives and to trust His plans for us.

PERSEVERE

Finally, it is important to consider that we need to persevere even when we are embattled. It sounds easy enough to help others and to be kind, but both the world and the enemy of our souls are working against us. The world wants us to become distracted by material things and short-term pleasures, and the enemy would like for us to give up entirely. This is why we are encouraged not to become "weary in doing good, for at the proper time we will reap a harvest if we do not give up" (Gal. 6:9). God knows that doing good things is challenging. We will face rejection, distractions, exhaustion, and other issues, but if we hang in there and continue to pursue God, we will have fruitful lives. Not perfect lives, but fruitful ones where we can and will make an impact on the world for things that matter eternally, and we will develop a heart for the things that matter to God, particularly His people of all nations.

FOOD FOR OUR SOULS

We are to be an expectant and ready people. Having a fruitful life is food for our souls. We feed our bodies with vegetables and breads, but we feed our souls with His purposes. "My food," said Jesus, "is to do the will of him who sent me and to finish his work. Do you not say, 'Four months more and then the harvest'? I tell you, open your eyes and look at the fields! They are ripe for harvest" (John 4:34–35). Go and pursue God's will in your life. I assure you that you will not be disappointed.

POINTS TO CONSIDER: HARVEST OF FRUITFULNESS

- When we choose God's will, we experience the fruit of joy.
- We can impact the world in a way that has eternal value.
- Both big and small, all tasks can be a fruitful blessing to others if it is where God is calling you.

EXPLORATION QUESTIONS

1. How can I seek fruitfulness in my spiritual life?
2. How is God leading me right now?
3. What first steps can I take toward God's direction for me?
4. What obstacles are hindering me from taking those steps?

FOCUS VERSE

As the rain and the snow come down from heaven, and do not return to it without watering the earth and making it bud and flourish, so that it yields seed for the sower and bread for the eater, so is my word that goes out from my mouth: It will not return to me empty, but will accomplish what I desire and achieve the purpose for which I sent it.

—Isaiah 55:10–11

PRAYER

Lord, thank You that you promise that I can have a fruitful life. Help me to rely on You and Your Word to guide my steps and to enable me to walk in Your ways. Help me to be concerned with things that have eternal value, and to allow Your Spirit to guide me. I pray You will help me to grow in the character traits that matter to You and to seek Your guidance and direction in my life as to the places You have prepared for me to be fruitful in. In Jesus' name, amen.

IF YOU WOULD LIKE TO START A RELATIONSHIP WITH JESUS:

This is a very important decision in your life and one I am confident you will not regret. You are not converting to a religion, but starting a personal relationship with Jesus as your Lord and Savior. He loves you more than you will ever know, and He will be with you in all of your joys and trials. He gives you the promise of His salvation through the presence of the Holy Spirit in your heart. You will learn to recognize His voice, and you will need to be in a community of believers who can care for you and encourage you to grow in your faith.

The first step is admitting that you are not able to avoid sinful attitudes and behaviors without the help of the Holy Spirit and the power of repentance. This is a step that requires you to let go of self-sufficiency and pride and to admit that you need God's love and His grace. The next step is to invite Him in to your heart and to start a relationship with Him. That means you talk with Him in prayer and you share your problems and hopes with Him as you would with a close friend. It is also important that you learn more about Him by reading the Bible and by attending a church where you can hear good biblical teaching and be in a community of believers. Please pray this prayer of invitation to start your journey.

PRAYER OF INVITATION

Dear Jesus, I don't know You very well yet, but I want to invite You into my heart today as an acknowledgement of trust and hope in Your promise of grace and love for me, even though I don't deserve it. Please receive my humble apology for living a life on my own of self-sufficiency and selfish desires. I need Your forgiveness and ask for You to heal my heart and lead me in Your ways. Teach me by Your Holy Spirit to understand You more, and help me to walk forward in a way that is pleasing to You. When I start to doubt and feel like giving up, please give me the strength to trust You and to trust in Your word. Thank You for making a way for me to know God and to experience Your grace first hand. I love You and thank You for coming into my heart and loving me. In Jesus' name, amen.

THE SERENITY PRAYER

God,
grant me the serenity to accept the things
I cannot change,
the courage to change the things I can,
and the wisdom to know the difference.
Living one day at a time;
accepting hardship as a pathway to peace;
taking, as Jesus did, this sinful world as it is;
not as I would have it;
trusting that You will make all things right
If I surrender to your will;
so that I may be reasonably happy in this life
And supremely happy with You forever in the next.
Amen.

—Reinhold Neibuhr

BIBLIOGRAPHY

Alcorn, Randy, *The Treasure Principle; Unlocking the Secret of Joyful Giving.* Multnomah Publishers Inc., 2001.

Bourne, Edmund J., Ph.D., *Anxiety and Phobia Workbook.* New Harbinger Publications, Inc., 1995.

Dr. Ellis, Albert, *Catastrophising, All or Nothing Thinking.* Secular Theorist who developed Rational Emotive Behavioral Therapy, 1973-2007.

George, Terry (director), *Hotel Rwanda,* 2004.

Keller, Phillip,W., *A Shepherd Looks at Psalm 23.* Daybreak Books, Zondervan Publishing House,1970, 70.

Lawrence, Brother, *The Practice of the Presence of God.* Whitaker House, 1982, 53.

Spurgeon, C.H, *All of Grace; The Infinite Love of God.* Whitaker House, 1983, 37.

Printed in the United States
127845LV00002B/1/P